Think & Grow

Confident

Acknowledgements

The author is an Accredited Life Coach and Neuro Linguistic Programming NLP Practitioner. Some information contained within this publication may be NLP related. For such information the author fully credits any and all contributors from all sources within, but not limited to the field of NLP, Neuro Semitics, Psychology, Theology and all others.
I would like to express my gratitude to my wife Lizelle for her love and support. Thank you also to my mentors who invest positive energy and time in me.

A Special than you to:

- To Go the Father, Son and The Holy Spirit who is the strength of my life.

- To my Father and role model Bishop Dr. S J Lloyd. Thank you for the powerful concluding thoughts herein.

- A special thank you to all other mentors I admire and respect for their wisdom.

I dedicate this book to my life partner Lizelle, my daughter's Is-Rael and Eden, and all woman of this planet. You have all you need living inside you.

Contents

Introduction

Think & Grow Confident is a book for people from all walks of life. The intention behind this book is to help improve one's ability to put on the attitude of confidence. Each chapter builds upon the previous one. We start by understanding what drives our ability to function successfully in this life. By taking a look at what confidence really is, we uncover just why we struggle with it and where our struggle originates. We also look at how to turn the tide by focusing on the right things. Lastly, we explore ideas into discovering our life's purpose and a simple approach to emotional intelligence. We finally look at 'on the go' confidence tips. The entire process has been designed to help you unlock your own strengths.

Why Think & Grow Confident?

If we understood the power we possess between our ears, life would be blissful for the most part. For some reason we fail to use the most powerful and most accessible super computer ever built to live a joyful and abundant life. If everybody had confidence we would live in a different world today. We would all go after what we wanted simply because we would believe we could achieve our goals. The world is filled with broken dreams, broken hopes and broken people who live with regret and the shame of never getting it, doing it, or being it.

The Author's Conviction

The world consists of many books containing within their covers abundant wisdom. People like Oprah Winfrey, Barack Obama, Dr. Phil, Nelson Mandela, TD Jakes, Jessie Jackson, Denzel Washington, Will Smith and countless others have used many wise and timeless principles to achieve their success. I plan to highlight the wise principles found in my personal favorite book of timeless wisdom; the Bible. In my view, the Bible scriptures provide enlightening principles of wisdom containing every possible scenario life can present to us. My personal awareness is based upon these precepts and the contact Jesus Christ. In my view he was the ultimate model of true Confidence; Competence and Humility boldly displayed. My hope is that as I have found wisdom in the principles of the scriptures, you too will discover new ideas and your true identity.

Final thoughts

At the end of this program you will have new ideas on how to make powerful mental changes. You will also be in a position to start the process of going after what you want. You have more than enough potential and life has more than enough possibilities to make even the impossible things possible in your life time. The New Choice dictionary defines the word confidence as a firm trust in; Faith, a Belief in one's own ability. Other words closely related to confidence are: Self-Assurance, Boldness, Sureness, Certainty, and Self-Reliance.

I believe this program offers a set of golden keys to help you unlock the best years of your life and the door to your Greater Life Purpose. We will not only be talking about confidence, but also about the most important aspects relating to the subject.

I believe there are two ways in which people relate to confidence.

First, there are those who pretend to be confident, but deep down inside crave for people's attention. They find themselves almost at a point of depression when they express themselves and people don't bother to look at them twice. This easily alters their mood, causing highs and lows in their emotional state and it takes them a while to return to normalcy. If this is you then you are the *pretender*. You take forever to make decisions and when you do, you always second guess yourself. You are at your most vulnerable when you are alone, because your own company makes you fidgety. You need to be around people to feel important and secure.

Second **are those who are always capable.** They enjoy their own company and are completely satisfied in their own presence. They have little internal conflict and their decisions are final. They don't really care what others have to say and always believe they are right even when proven wrong. They are sometimes considered to be cold and selfish and often end up as the only player on their team. If this is you then you are the *defender*. You achieve great things, but make expensive mistakes because of your "Know it All" Attitude. You are at your most vulnerable when control is taken away from you. This is when your insecurity spikes and you mess up relationships. You need to be in control to feel important and secure.

None of the above is true confidence. To get to a place of true confidence requires effort on a physical, emotional and psychological level.

It is crucial to also understand that **confidence is not** arrogance. Kent Sayre says "*arrogance is a sign of insecurity*". Wherever the 'I' factor is present you will find arrogance in people. Some people are rude and try to hide behind candor. When people act in this way they display their lack of emotional intelligence. Take note; I said 'Act', because people are not their behavior, they act against their inner beliefs. This is one of the most liberating statements you will ever encounter. *People are not their behavior*.

Just by changing our beliefs, we can change our behavior patterns and change our lives. Read, listen, take part and be changed by renewing your mind. Shall we...?

Chapter One: Think

"As a man thinks in his Heart, So is he" The Bible

We spend time taking care of our health, our life, our love life, our career life, our social life and our family life, but we seldom consider investing in our **Thought Life**. Our thought life is an independent life from which all things originate. Our Heart or Mind State is our thought life. Everything is conceived within our thoughts. Our thought life is our seed and our material experience, the harvest of our seed. When our thought life is pure, good and positive it will produce pure, good and positive life experiences; after its own kind.

Our thoughts produce things

God blessed them and said, "Be fertile, increase in number, fill the earth, and be its master. Rule the fish in the sea, the birds in the sky, and all the animals that crawl on the earth". The Bible

The mind is fertile enough to achieve any thought invested in it. The thoughts we have, will increase in number and fill the earth without our consent. At every stage of our lives our thinking will produce an outcome. Life is centered on producing after our own kind. What kind? The kind of thoughts we have. You and I produce after our own thoughts. The kind of thoughts we harbor will ultimately determine our life experience.

Think with me for a moment; the chair you are sitting on now was first a thought. Your cellphone was a thought. The software running the cellphone was a thought. The car you drive, the plane you fly and the electricity we enjoy today, were all thoughts. Your job, your relationships; your children were all thoughts produced after their own kind. So is low self-esteem, depression, frustration, hate, anger, fear and other negative emotions. All these emotions emanate from thoughts and I will prove this to you.

Let's do a quick experiment.

I want you think of a person who really irritates you. Someone who disappoints you, someone who's hurt you. Now close your eyes and think of this person for the next 15 seconds.

How do you feel?

Write the feeling down: _____

Now I want you to think of someone you really love, someone who makes you happy, someone who fills you with joy. Now close your eyes and think of them for the next 15 seconds.

How do you feel?

Write the feeling down: _____

Where did the feelings come from? Your thoughts are things. Was the person there? No But by now you understand how much energy springs from your thoughts. Think of how you feel when you think of these people and how the energy, negative or positive, increases when you think about them.

"Thoughts are Things, and powerful things at that, when they are mixed with definiteness of purpose, persistence, and a burning desire will translate into riches, or other material objects". Napolian Hill

Our thoughts will produce after their kind. Our thinking produces, but our feelings multiply.

Our Thoughts Preserve Life

"If you're not thinking, you are deteriorating" NMC.

Have you ever considered your body temperature regulates itself while you are sleeping? While you're asleep and getting hot; your brain (*The Thinking Tool*) will tells your arms to remove the blanket. If you get too hot, you could suffer from panic attacks or even worse; heat strokes. Babies can't regulate their body temperature, so the babies cry when they are uncomfortable with the temperature. Your human thinking is fully developed when the brain is able to link messages from your senses to your brain while asleep. Your senses will send a message to the brain communicating that you are too hot, and the brain will respond by instructing the arms to remove the covers and improve the temperature. In short; if you can do this, you are a Genius.

Burk Esterhuyse writes the following in his book **The User Manual to the Mind**.

The Thinking Tool (Your Brain)

• 98% of our knowledge about human brain has been learned in last 10   years!
• 80% of everything scientists knew about brain by 1990 is today proven to be false!

Modern technology and new devices make it possible for researchers to continue beyond what we ever thought possible before. As a result our knowledge will continue to expand, our perceptions will continually change. This will impact all aspects of our world including the medical and wellness industries.

Think about it, until 1990 doctors were taught that our brain is hard-wired. Thanks to modern science and devices developed, we can now monitor the human brain while still alive; seeing exactly which part of the brain is involved in which functions. This is how they discovered the brain is not hard-wired! It can change, create new neural pathways, make new connections, retract the old ones, etc. This is called 'brain plasticity'.

We also learned our thoughts are real! It's not just a thought; it's a material thing, made of energy (they are bio-electrical and biochemical impulses) and better yet, they are the most potent energy known to us!

10 Truths about your Powerful Brain:

1. When 10% dehydrated, it's 50% less efficient!
2. It has a total of 160,000 kilometers of blood vessels.
3. It is always on; it never rests throughout your whole life.
4. One brain cell is more sophisticated than the entire world's telephone networks.
5. We were not born hard-wired; we can change behaviors and make new neural connections.
6. Consist of more than 100 Billion neurons; as many stars are in the Milky Way.
7. Everyone possesses a natural Genius ability.
8. Is Capable of 10 000 Trillion operations per second.
9. We are limitless in capacity to learn and grow fast!
10. At least 1000 times faster than the fastest supercomputer in the world.

Source: Burk Esterhuyse - The User Manual to the Mind

You Are Genius Already, Use your "Thinking Tool"

When we understand how powerful we are and how we can use our thinking tool to change, life, as we know it, alters forever. We communicate with our subconscious mind through our thoughts and senses. This is how we send negative messages to our subconscious mind; which beneath the surface will produce (the negative message) after its own kind by conspiring with the universe around us. The universe will multiply our feelings into our living experience.

For example: I go for a job interview and I want to be positive. I tell myself I am positive and claim I am the best candidate for the job, but deep down in me I really don't believe it. This belief triggers an uncomfortable vibration. If the feeling (vibration) is doubt or fear, the interviewer or review panel will feel the negative vibration when assessing my application and doubt me or have fear of hiring me; a product of my doubt!. This is how these thoughts will produce results.

Feelings are more important than words. We can convince ourselves with words that we are positive until we are blue, but if we don't believe it, with the way we feel (vibration), it will not happen. Why? Our sub-conscience produces thoughts and feelings after its own kind.

What we described till now is the power of thoughts working in our lives. We can't medicate the symptoms of this problem. Medicating the symptoms is like giving someone with a flu virus a vitamin c capsule, when they really need an antibiotic to kill the virus first and then boost their immune system. We should learn to cure the root of the problem. All problems start in our thought life and in order to solve them we need to change the way we conduct our thought life.

Prioritized Thinking

Priorities are simply the order in which we attend to our responsibilities. In other words: what should be prior to what, or putting first things first. Thinking is our first and most important responsibility. The right question to ask is, "what should be first?" The answer being "Think before you do." A recent survey showed 91 % of people, who took out impulse short-term debt such as personal loans, regretted not thinking about whether they really needed it or whether it would be gratifying to have the extra cash. They said they could probably manage without it, if their priorities were reshuffled. How many times do we do things without thinking it through? How many products have we bought in the spur of the moment and later wish we hadn't? We make silly mistakes as a result of not taking a moment to think before we do.

A single mother by the name of Mary worked for a major retail bank as a teller. She was approached by a man on her lunch break one afternoon with an offer to make an easy $1,000. All she had to do was to alert him via a text message when someone made a substantial withdrawal over $5,000. Desperate to buy medicine for her sick son and without thinking she agreed. Mary was an honest woman who never committed a crime before. She went back in, observed one of the business customers withdrawing a large sum of money and sent a text message to the man the moment a gentlemen left.

What she didn't know was the man who approached her was an undercover agent investigating a string of muggings and robberies related to the same bank she was working for. They knew there was a link inside the bank. Her colleague Jessica was the link to a criminal network all along but Mary was arrested immediately and later convicted and sentence to 10 years in prison. Jessica was never arrested.

Mary should've thought about it, but like many of us she invested little in her thought life. She never thought things through and paid dearly for it. If we can take 30 seconds to consider why we should and why we shouldn't in every situation, we will be better off. So take 30 seconds and think about it.

Prioritize the right thoughts

"Fix your thoughts on what is true, honorable, right, pure, lovely, and admirable. Think about things that are excellent and worthy of praise". The Bible

Now that we understand we ought to think first we should move on to what to think on. It is always best to prioritize the right productive thoughts over the wrong unproductive thoughts. As we said before; priorities are simply the order in which we decide responsibilities. We already know our thought life produce our living experiences and that our subconscious mind multiplies our thoughts and feelings into things, but we ought to know there is power in reshaping our thought priorities. In other words; we should rethink what we think about and place the importance of positive thoughts over negative ones.

The 20/80 Principle

Dr. John Maxwell shares his insight on the Perato Principle in his book; *Developing the Leader within You*. He explains how 20% of the staff in a company produces 80% of the business income. My take on the Perato Principle A.K.A the 20/80 Principle is that 80% of our work should be Mind Work and 20% physical. Mind work refers to our thinking, planning, strategy, creative considerations and other forms of productive thinking. Physical work refers to the *"implementing"* of ideas. If we begin to spend as much time thinking on the right priorities as we do on entertaining ourselves, we would blossom in every area of our lives. Anyone who has a passive real estate income will tell you that 80% of the work was done when the real estate was purchased. The Mind work involved thinking, planning, negotiating and setting up the property for tenants to move in. After all that, only 20% remain in maintaining and managing the investment.

Critical thinking

The American Philosophical Association has defined critical thinking as "the process of purposeful, self-regulatory judgment". The process gives reasoned consideration to evidence, contexts, conceptualizations, methods, and criteria" (The American Philosophical Association 1990). Critical thinking is sometimes broadly defined as "thinking about thinking."

Criticism comes to mind when I think of critical thinking. Criticism can actually be a positive approach. This may sound negative, but in reality critical thinking is a powerful tool that can be used to interrogate conceptions. It is what keeps businesses from going under, what keeps relationships intact and what keeps us "thinking straight". Critical thinking is a method of thinking in which reasonable time is taken to criticize the detail of an idea. The purpose of this method is to sift the relevant truth. Without engaging critical thinking we would live in a society of stupor instead of common sense.

Can you imagine a world where everything was just accepted and nothing was interrogated? Critical thinking gives us the opportunity to view things in a way that promotes sense over non-sense. This method allows us the privilege to investigate opportunities and pitfalls alike.

My mom is quite a critical thinker. She is a brilliant judge of character as she is always critically engaged, taking nothing at face value. This approach has saved her time and time again from the evil intentions of other people. I'm not encouraging suspicion, but critical thinking. Critical thinking should always lead to discovery and serve as an interpretation of underlying intentions.

I once advertised a smart cellphone on Gumtree the South African version of EBay. A guy called me and said he was interested in the phone. He then asked about my bank and I told him that I was banking with ABSA and he said that he was banking with FNB. In our country inter-bank transfers take at least two to days to clear, but the proof of payment is instant via mobile phone text. I then decided to open an FNB account so that the money would immediately reflect in my account. After this I called him and updated him on the bank account and he proposed we meet at a petrol station in Orange Grove. He then said he had two business accounts, a Nedbank and FNB account, but he couldn't meet me as he was tied up somewhere and he would send his brother.

My suspicions were aroused when 'his brother' came walking. He called me at the garage and asked to speak to the brother probably to confirm if the phone was in order. A minute later I got a phone text from 'Nedbank' advising the money had been paid. I reluctantly handed the phone over and the 'brother' left. About 300 yards from me he raced away and disappeared among the houses. After seeing this, a rush of doubt came over me. My instincts were to take the phone text number and Google it. When I got to the office I immediately googled the number and to my dismay I got the shock of my life when the search came back as 'scam', 'scam', 'scam'. I tried calling the number in vain and the phone just rang and rang until it was completely switched off. These people robbed me in broad daylight. I just sat there for literally half an hour and couldn't believe what had just happened to me.

As I pondered on the events of the day I realized the many mistakes I made. I did not thoroughly interrogate the situation. My desperation for the money clouded my will to interrogate all the facts and I didn't ask critical questions, I was way too trusting. My mother would never have done this; she would reason and investigate until she was satisfied. There were so many red flags like the bank accounts, the rendezvous to exchange the goods, and the 'brother' who didn't look like he represented a businessman. I never criticized the motives of these people and the price for my haste was a high. It cost me a $500 smartphone, a powerful life lesson on critical thinking and a lesson on listening to my intuition.

When do I need to think critically?

- When it seems that something is too good to be true.
- When you are too excited with an idea.

Never make decisions on the spur of the moment. Criticize the whole thing in your mind.

Our ability to think determines usefulness.

In a recent survey conducted by InterSearch Worldwide and published in the Search-Consult magazine, it was found that the number one skill a successful CEO should possess, is the ability to think strategically. Our reality is ultimately the evidence of our thinking...

We can't be anything *unless we thought to be it first.*

We can't do anything *unless we thought to do it first.*

We can't go anywhere unless we first see ourselves there in our thoughts.

Our thoughts are the first steps on the journey there. (**NMC**)

Conclusion

"*The ancestor of every action is a thought*".

Ralph Waldo Emerson

As we develop our Thinking, we ultimately become the very thing we think about. Therefore one cannot separate action from the original state of ancestry, which is a thought. Thought sets every life cycle in motion. Whatsoever you Think, you Become. *(Bishop Dr. SJ Lloyd)*

Chapter Two: Confidence is an Attitude

"Confidence is A Mind Attitude expressed when we boldly display Competence and Humility at the same time" (NMC)

The word attitude is described in the dictionary as a manner of thought or feeling. Attitude is all about how we project our thoughts and feelings to others. How do others know what our thoughts are? By what we say and how we say it. How does the other person know how we feel? The expression on our face and our body language speaks louder than our voices.

A wise person knows when and how to put on the attitude of confidence. A person who has not yet learned when and how to put on the attitude of confidence, really doesn't- believe they have any shred of confidence at all. We all possess a natural ability to put it on, like we would put on sunscreen and believe we are protected from the UV Rays of the sun, so is the attitude of confidence when we put it on.

Confidence is internal

True confidence doesn't come from external factors, but from internal convictions. The word conviction is derived from the concept of being convinced about something. What are you convinced about when it comes to the way you think of your-self? Think about this carefully. The convictions you live by will either increase or decrease your attitude of confidence.

Convictions are here to serve us, either for our good or our bad, but ultimately our conviction is our own choice. We allow ourselves to be convinced about one thing or another. People who spend many years behind bars come out and find it hard to adjust to society. I know someone who spent 17 years in prison and when he got out found it really hard to adjust his mind to the outside world. He told himself he would not make it; he would never survive the outside world. When he got out he was lucky enough to get a job, but in less than 3 months on the job, he received three warnings for his conduct and was eventually fired.

The most important daily conversation is the one we have with ourselves. "I am sick, I am unlucky, and I am always late". After a while our thought life adopts this as truth and produces this as reality .We then walk in these experiences as a result of our thinking. At this stage the conviction that I am sick or unlucky or always late is a reality and this scenario repeats itself.

In the same way when we tell ourselves enough times we are not beautiful, the mind creates a pattern of the feeling and it soon becomes automatic. After a while we don't even have to say anything to ourselves anymore, because our subconscious mind has made our thoughts about ourselves a reality. We've now created a monster, a conviction in our mind. Whatever our mind believes, will be reflected in our living experience. Our mind is the most powerful part of us and will convince others of what we are already convinced about; I am not beautiful. Our attitude is very much related to our perception about ourselves; a perception so strong, people around us perceive the same thing.

"Life is 10% what happens to me and 90% how I react to it"

John Maxwell

"No matter what the situation, you choose your reaction, assigning meaning and value to an event. ... You either teach people to treat you with dignity and respect, or you don't". Dr. Phil

I project only what I am. People don't buy products or companies or even experts, but people buy people. People don't buy what you say, but subconsciously they buy what you express through body language. We all sell ourselves daily and our biggest selling point by far is always our attitude.

The one thing I always consider when hiring staff is their attitude before, during and after an interview. Overconfidence to me is conceitedness and under confidence exposes one's lack of surety in one's ability, but the right attitude is when there is a perfect balance between Competence and Humility, and Boldness.

Honesty also plays a big role within confidence. A person who tries to over promise, or over compensate always spells trouble. They are often not aware their dishonest behavior is evident through their vibration. 99% of people know when someone is trying to con them. It is a natural thing for people to sense dishonesty since we all have intuition. Some of us act on our intuition and some don't, but we all know at some level when there is an ulterior motive. Some people are just plainly suspicious, but for the most part we all have an active intuition.

I remember a conversation with one of my previous business mentors. He's probably one of the greatest sales people I've ever met and I have a lot of respect for him. We were on our way to meet one of the corporate giants and whilst driving, we were talking about quality case studies to show prospective clients. Anytime we were to pitch to a client we needed to present case studies showing our expertise and effectiveness.

He said something that disappointed me somewhat. I asked him what we would do if we did not have the relevant information to supply our prospective clients. His answer sent shock waves down my spine. He replied "*We make it up*" and like you, I was in shock and couldn't believe my ears.

Some people are so good convincing themselves something exists; they could even sell the same nonexistent idea to someone else who in their innocence believes them. That is a dangerous place to be and I never want to get there. It will catch up with you and it will cost you dearly, keep your integrity intact!. Don't prostitute yourself for any material thing no matter how desperate you may be or how great the need is. Dignity and a clean conscience are far more important and valuable than any deal or any amount of money. Sleeping peacefully at night is worth more than all riches in the world. Money can buy you an expensive and comfortable bed but cannot buy you a minute of sleep.

One thing separates good communicators from brilliant ones; their attitude. Even the waiter's tip in a restaurant is always determined by *their manner of thought* and *body language*. Not too long ago a waiter spilled mushroom sauce all over me and I was furious to say the least, but he gave a genuine apology with sincerity and that calmed me down.

"*Your attitude will determine your altitude*" Author Unknown

The difference between who gets my sale in the shop or at the car dealership is the attitude of the sales person. I never buy from conceited individuals who want to show me that they are smarter than me. I always look for the most helpful person and end up buying from them, because they have the right manner of thought and body language. Attitude also has a great deal to do with the way you approach a person or situation. The right attitude is being approachable in the first place, putting the other person ahead of yourself.

A friend of mine went to a car dealership some years ago wearing nothing more than a pair of shorts, a t-shirt and a pair of sneakers. He walked into the showroom where the new cars were displayed and was approached by one of the sales people. The sales guy looked at him with a prejudicial attitude and asked "*Can I Help You Sir?*" Not, Good Day or a Hi, just a 'let's get on to business you don't belong here' attitude. My friend replied; "*Yes, I would like to test drive the new VW GTI.* The sales person with disgust all over his face said, "*Unfortunately we don't have any cars at the moment they are all out. Do you perhaps have a pay slip with you; we can check in the meantime if you qualify*"? Qualify? How was that relevant? Don't you have the right to like something before you decide to buy it? And how will you know if you like it if you have not been exposed to it?

My friend did this on purpose to prove a point, so he wasn't upset at all; he just felt vindicated and replied "*No, I am buying cash*" and showed the sales person his bank statement. You can imagine how small the sales guy felt at this point as his jaw dropped and he was in complete shame and regret. My friend said to him "*never judge a book by its cover.*" He approached another sales person, test drove and paid for the car that very day.

Conceitedness can cost us dearly, especially when we mistake it for confidence. Confidence is not displayed by insulting or belittling the next person. True confidence is reflected when the next person feels respected and important after we've dealt with them.

In this manner we display true confidence (the right balance between competence and humility, and boldness) when we make others feel important. Growing up I always heard the old people say *"respect goes a long way."*

Our Words

"It is the spirit that gives life; the flesh profits nothing: the words that I speak unto you, they are spirit, and they are life". The Bible

In other words everything I say is in a good spirit and to preserve life. Whatever we say must always be in good spirit (keeping the peace) and to add light (life) to the situation.

Ever heard the saying *"the pen is mightier than the sword?"* Words pierce deeper into the soul than any weapon can. Words have the ability to break, to heal, to restore dignity, to show respect, to change attitudes and even to change our hearts.

It was the words *"Yes We Can"* that inspired the new belief in America to elect Barack Obama as the first African-American president in history. Words inspire change.

Two word groups either improve our attitude or depress our attitude. These are constructive words and destructive words.

Think about what happens when someone tells you a story? The words they use will determine how you respond to the story. In the mind words become pictures, pictures become feelings and feelings are what we project on to others. Have you ever been in a situation where things are alive and happening at a family gathering or an office function, all of a sudden someone comes in and says something that changes the atmosphere? I'm sure you've experience something similar before.

Constructive words are positive words. When you use positive words, you project a positive atmosphere, the right atmosphere produces positive results.

Destructive words are negative words and will produce a negative atmosphere with disastrous results.

Serena Williams was at her lowest point in her career in early 2011, when she spent months in recovery at home. She was overwhelmed by a depressing series of health scares, sending her to the hospital repeatedly and keeping her away from tennis for almost a year. Serena, a former No. 1 in world tennis whose ranking slid to 175th made history after feeling a twinge of self-doubt connected to her quick exit at the French Open. She was beaten by a woman ranked 111th. This was Williams' only first-round loss in 48 major tournaments.

Serena Williams surprised the world when she returned to Wimbledon progressing to the final with ease. She started well in the final, but somehow in the middle lost her way. "*I just got too anxious,*" she said, "*and I shouldn't have been so anxious.*", but suddenly Williams regained control down the stretch and produced a 16 stroke point with a forehand put away to get to break point.

"*After that, I remember thinking, I can definitely do this!*" Williams said. She pushed through breaking her opponent's serve several times, applying pressure and teaching the youngster how champions play tennis. Serena went on to win the 2012 Wimbledon final at the age of 30, making her the oldest women's singles champion at any major tournament since Martina Navratilova won Wimbledon at age 33 in 1990. This was Serena's 14th major title, ending a two-year drought.

What amazed me were the words she spoke over herself: "*I can definitely do this!* ". At the most difficult time of the match, the right words were crucial. Serena spoke life at the darkest but most important moment in her life and career. By speaking to herself and reminding herself what she was capable of, she instilled a new belief within and used positive words, to stimulate positive pictures, and positive pictures to spur up positive feelings. Her positive attitude regained her championship for her.

Again I ask you, what conversations do you have with your-self? It's never too late for a comeback; you can still win in the game of life.

Body Language

Ever heard the saying *"First impressions are lasting impressions"*? There are some people who walk in a room and say absolutely nothing, but still make their presence felt. These selected few understand confidence to go far more than words. It's called Non-verbal Communication and it's probably one of the biggest scientific breakthroughs in the study of human communication.

People with a Non-verbal Presence command your attention on a subconscious level and attract attention because of how they present themselves. You can't really put your finger on what it is about the person, but there is something different about them. What really attract people to these non-verbal masters are the convictions they have about themselves. They know their enormous potential and see the possibilities for their lives. They are blissfully aware off their unfailing appetite for growth and success. The good news is that you and I possess the same surety inside of us; we just have to learn to access and master it.

Present your-self for where you are going, not where you are.

Have you ever been to a place where you appeared overdressed? You don't fit in because this is not your only destination. When you are going to the motor mechanic dressed in formal clothing perhaps to get something repaired, you are the odd one out amongst all the grease monkeys; however the garage is not the last place you were going as you might have other appointments after.

Preparation is about preparing in your mind for where your physical body has not yet been. When you get to your final destination, you will be confident as you have been there before, mentally. Preparation is 90% mental and 10% physical. First work the detail out in your mind. For instance: What you need to do, why you need to do it, how you need to do it, when you need to it and the immediate steps to take. When your thinking becomes your work, the physical work is 90% less strenuous.

"Work your mind, not your behind" Rev Ike.

Balance

One of my father's dearest friends Dr. David Demas once spoke about the four P's. The four P's are Preparation Prevents Poor Presentation. We just spoke about working your mind; however it is important to work with your mind in how you appear. People don't see your mind, but how you present what is on your mind. Therefore it is important to look at that part.

Buy a few new outfits and you involuntarily move into a different dress consciousness. What we wear is a reflection of our thinking. If you are striving to be an entrepreneur or work in a business environment, it is crucial to understand the following principle.

"People like people who are like themselves". NLP Quote

When business people look at you, they want to see themselves. Simply put; people like people they can identify with. This boosts your attitude and makes you feel even more confident, because not only are you prepared to share your ideas, but your appearance communicates that you can deliver those brilliant ideas. When you get ready to meet with investors or to approach your boss for an increase or a different job, dress for success.

Conclusion

"The greatest discovery of any generation is that a human being can alter his life by altering his attitude"
William James.

A positive attitude sets you up for greatness. The first step to true confidence is learning to alter our attitude. When we master our attitudes, we can begin to live a meaningful and prosperous life. As we alter our attitude so we need to alter our appearance by dressing the part. This will reflect our attitude as that of confidence and bring us closer to greater doors. (*Bishop Dr. SJ Lloyd*)

Chapter Three: Your Greatest Enemy

"Your strength is determined by the size of your opposition". NMC

In order to conquer your enemy, you must understand the strengths and weaknesses of your enemy. The first question we should ask ourselves is; who is my greatest enemy? The answer will shock you and you will find the answer in a very familiar place. Go to the nearest mirror you can find and ask the person looking back at you; who is your greatest enemy? Then look away and look at the mirror again until you can answer the question honestly.

As you gather by now, the answer has nothing to do with anything or anyone outside you; it has everything to do with you. Your greatest enemy is your *Insecurity*. Yes! Your insecurity is the biggest obstacles in your life and will continue to rob you and I of the greatness we have until we decide to conquer this, our greatest enemy. Our insecurities are built upon our constant negative self-thoughts, self-talk and the fact that we allow the negative opinions of others have to affects us. Insecurities occur when your thought life is out of place.

How many times does the approval of others have more say than your own genius ideas? When did you decide your own unique taste for clothes, food, decor, cars or anything is wrong and the opinions of others are better than yours? I want to tell you, you can cut this monster down to size and start holding your own. Do you want to take your life back or continue living your life through the eyes of your oppressors? Yes, I said oppressors.

"Anything or anyone who does not support your own uniqueness and causes you to doubt your-self is an oppressor in your life". NMC

Fear is an Oppressor

An oppressor will weigh you down and crush your will to live until you give up on your hopes and dreams. An oppressor will force you into hiding your brilliance and convince you that you cannot go higher than where you are. Fear is the fuel of insecurity making it the biggest oppressor in our lives. One of the clearest definitions I've heard on fear is: *False Evidence Appearing Real.* Fear appears to be real, but is not real. The only place where fear is real is in the mind. Can you see a ghost? No. Is the ghost real? Yes, in the mind? Can you live your best life when you learn to confront your fears? Absolutely Yes! No oppressor can rule over you forever.

Fear of Rejection

The fear of rejection is a self-imagined fear. This fear exists in your mind. The more you think of the fear, the stronger becomes the vibration you send out to the universe and the universe will in turn give you more of the same through your experience *(The Law of Attraction JC Maxwell).* Our life experiences act as triggers for insecurities. The triggers such as bad memories can creep up on us and harm us if we don't effectively deal with them. Our fears are stationed in the subconscious mind. We have to resolve it here to relieve these triggers of power to confuse and overwhelm us.

- How many times do we find we are afraid to go into a new relationship as the fear of what happened in last one still lives within?

- How many people are afraid of re-entering the business arena because their previous business experience was bitter and caused so much pain and discomfort?

- How many children fear they will never be loved, because they have been told over and over they are not worth loving? Many of these children are now adults with the same fears.

- How many children fail repeatedly because they have been told they are not good enough, smart enough or good-looking enough and these children believe this, thus creating the fear of rejection?

We now understand fear to be the oppressor that ruins lives. Not one person on earth was born with fear, not even you. If you were indeed born with fear; how is it possible for a one year old toddler to leap from the bed in to the arms of the parent without warning? They never considered the possibility they might fall. They are without fear.

- **Self-rejection**- "I don't think I can do it". You reject yourself.

- **Outside-rejection**- "What if they don't like me?" When you think others will reject you.

- **Self-pity** "people never listen to what I have to say, I'll just wait until someone decides to hear me out". When you are sorry for yourself, because you don't believe others will give you attention unless you behave in this way.

The above fears never support your goals, ambitions and dreams. Fear never supports your own uniqueness. The fear of rejection keeps your best intentions locked up inside you, convincing you, you are inadequate to achieve greatness. These fears make us believe that we don't deserve any better. This oppressor suppresses your self-belief making it difficult to have a confident outlook on life. Fear is a weight dragging you down and crippling you. Fear fuels our insecurity and the more you believe in the fear the more it becomes real, impacting your life in a miserable way.

Understanding Our Anxieties

Anxiety occurs when we become nervous about what we expect from ourselves. Ever noticed when you're anxious, you feel helpless and can't really put your finger on what's bothering you? That's because we want to be in control and when we can't be in control we become nervous. We also want to do something about the way we feel, especially when it comes to dealing with this emotion. We literally lose our minds over something we can't control. Yes, we can be silly, but for some people this is a real problem. As people, we don't always like to be stretched, we would rather be comfortable. Life has a way of making us uncomfortable and stretching us.

Anxiety is also one of the oppressors we have to deal with. Think of a parent constantly selling fear to a child. When a child is constantly warned (in caution I almost want to say intimidated) by one parent with another saying things like; "just wait until your father comes home" or "I'm going to tell your father", the child feels helpless and becomes anxious. Often the treatments we give children shape their capacity to put on the attitude of confidence. As a parent, I do not believe in driving fear into a child, but being stern and loving with clear communication. I think it's important to focus on the message, not the mess.

We must at all costs, balance our stern approach in warning children about their behavior and what the consequences will be where it concerns the other parent. "Just wait until your father comes home" can also create a negative perception about the other parent in the eyes of the child and all they see is monster coming to punish them. It's not the stern warnings driving the anxiety, but not knowing what to expect. Ever had an HIV test? Then you know how it feels to be in that position. We feel helpless as there's nothing we can do accept wait. We feed our minds with anxiety by thinking compulsively about our negative expectations. We only see the monster and not the other possibilities in the situation. We have to learn to relax and let life take its course. Come to your own rescue and start thinking on what is positive in the situation. When we do this, the monster becomes smaller and smaller.

When I conduct Braintools seminars I often take the participants on a journey. We teach them the power of imagination by taking them on an imaginary road trip. On this trip we feed them imaginary foods and 99% of them always tell me how they tasted vanilla ice cream; one of the foods on the imaginary food list. When we are done imagining the scenario, they open their eyes and I ask them, "*Was it real, what did you experience*"? They all reply saying it felt so real and that they could taste vanilla ice cream. They always crave for ice cream afterwards. That is the power of the mind.

"*What the mind of man can conceive and believe, it can achieve"* Napoleon Hill

The following account illustrates how powerful the mind is

I heard a story some years ago of a man called Nick Sitzman who was traveling across America by sneaking from one freight train to the next. One night he climbed into what he thought was a boxcar. He closed the door, which automatically locked shut and trapped him inside. When his eyes adjusted to the light, he realized he was inside a refrigerated boxcar, and he became aware of the intense, freezing cold.

He called for help and pounded on the door, but all the noise he made from the inside of the box car failed to attract anyone's attention. After many hours of struggle, he lay down on the floor of the railroad car. As he tried to fight against the freezing cold, he scratched a message on the floor explaining his unfortunate, imminent death. Late the next day, repairmen from the railroad opened the door and found the dead man inside. Though the man appeared to be frozen to death, the truth was the repairmen had come to fix the broken refrigerator unit in that car. Most likely the temperature of the railroad car had never fallen below fifty degrees during the night. The man had died because he *thought* he was freezing to death. This is the power of False Evidence Appearing Real. Nick Sitzman convinced himself he was getting cold and the freezer was on. He died as a result of his own fear oppressing him.

"For God has not given you a Spirit of Fear, but of Love, Self-Control and of a Sound Mind". The Bible

- *Love* has no fear attached, love is free and anything that makes you feel trapped is not love. Fear is a trap.
- *Self-control* is our ability to have emotional intelligence, Control how, what, and when we respond to our emotions and the emotions of others.
- When we start accepting we have *Sound Mind* (a stable mind more than capable to deal with and master the issues of life), we can appreciate and use the power of choice.

How many times do we create something out of nothing? What we don't understand is our fear is a vibration sent out into the universe to accomplish a certain goal and the goal is to bring whatever your energy was focused on. If you believe you are getting worse, you will get worse. It's not sickness that kills people, its fear that kill people. People create their own destiny with their negative self-talk, sending negative vibrations, which in turn creates the very fear they have. If you believe you will die from cancer, guess what, you will die from cancer. Even stronger; if you fear you will get cancer, you will get cancer. Vibration is energy and energy begets the same energy. Our insecurities are like a loaded gun just waiting for the right moment to destroy. Remember the guy who froze himself to death while the refrigerator was broken and the temperature was 50 degrees that night. He had a loaded gun.

Take a moment to reflect on the passage written by Marian Williamson on fear:

"Our deepest fear is not that we are inadequate. Our deepest fear is that we are powerful beyond measure. It is our light, not our darkness that most frightens us.' We ask ourselves, who am I to be brilliant, gorgeous, talented, and fabulous? Actually, who are you not to be? You are a child of God. Your playing small does not serve the world. There's nothing enlightened about shrinking so that other people won't feel insecure around you. We are all meant to shine, as children do. We were born to make manifest the glory of God that is within us. It's not just in some of us; it's in everyone. And as we let our own light shine, we unconsciously give others permission to do the same. As we are liberated from our own fear, our presence automatically liberates others".

A family we know experienced an incident where the father in the family was involved in a motor cycle crash early one Sunday morning. He was lucky to survive the crash, but was rushed to the emergency room and eventually spent several weeks in the Intensive Care Unit. I said to his daughter, "Wende, when you visit your dad, tell him every day, daddy every time I see you, you are looking better and better". She did just that and saw him recover as she said it daily. When she said to him he's looking better and better, he heard her and saw himself getting better. He eventually thought his way to his health and today is as healthy as Stallion at his advanced age. Now imagine if this is the power of a positive thought, how much power negative thoughts carry? In the same way when you tell a child that they are ugly or useless; the child grows up to be an adult with insecurities.

Fear leads to Stress

Stress is often the result of prolonged tension, anxiousness (Related to the Fear of something), irritability or trouble sleeping. Stress also hampers your ability to be clear, calm and to reason effectively. Stress is often pressure related making you doubt your abilities when it really matters. If stress is not adequately relieved, one can lose years of health by attracting chronic illnesses that affect the balance of a healthy body and mind.

"Anything or anyone who does not support your own uniqueness and causes you to doubt your-self is an oppressor in your life". (NMC)

In a recent study conducted in Sweden, scientists found people who said they were under permanent psychological stress for the previous year or longer, were three times more likely to have a stroke than those who said they were not. Stress like everything in our lives is a choice we make.

In my view, stress is an *"Idea"* we give power to in our lives. This idea becomes bigger with our words and actions and ultimately influences how we deal with the pressures of life. When we allow the priorities of daily life to become more important than our life and health, there is concern as we now enter dangerous territory. 90% of the time we don't even realize or understand how stress can impact our lives to the point of sickness and even a nervous system shut down. The body doesn't distinguish between physical and psychological threats. When you're stressed over a busy schedule, an argument with a friend, traffic, financial worries or something else your body reacts just as strongly as if you were facing a life-or-death situation.

If you have a lot of responsibilities and worries, your emergency stress response may be 'on' most of the time. The more your body's stress system is activated, the easier it is to trip and the harder it is to shut off. Chronic stress disrupts nearly every system in your body. It can raise blood pressure, suppress the immune system, increase the risk of heart attack, interfere with the body's pancreatic functions causing diabetes, stroke, contribute to infertility, and speed up the aging process. Long-term stress can even rewire the brain, leaving you more vulnerable to anxiety and depression.

How serious is Stress?

Stress can actually progress the cause of a stroke. There are three types of strokes related to stress: Large Vessel Disease (LVD) stroke, Small Vessel Disease (SVD) stroke, Cardio Embolic (CE) stroke and Cryptogenic stroke is a medical mystery with no known cause. A stroke is caused when the normal flow of blood to a part of your brain is suddenly cut off through blood clots.

When we become tense, anxious, angry, and irritable or have a lack of sleep, your body's natural emergency mode kicks in producing all kinds of emergency functions that can actually make you sick, as your body tries to protect you from what it considers as outsiders. In other words, stress is foreign and we must find relief.

How to reduce Stress

To reduce your stress levels as much as possible start by making exercise a priority and working out at least 20 minutes a day, sharing responsibilities at home and at work, and eating a healthy, balanced diet, rich in fruit and vegetables and start implementing quiet time (become silent, relax and take deep breaths for 20 minutes a day). This will help your body to increase blood flow to your brain and reduce the risk of blood clots in your brain. This will start your road to recovery and reduce your stress.

Source: Dr. Karen Woo from Bupa and also Helpguide.org

What can we do about Fear?

"Guard your heart above all else, for it determines the course of your life".

The Bible

We use our powerful mind to make choices all the time. By choosing we either guard or expose our heart. When we make good choices we guard our Heart, but when we make negative choices we expose ourselves to negative experiences, which always contribute to low morale and depressed self-belief.

The right choice we need to make is to guard our Heart. In other words we should learn how to guard our mindset. This is where we fight the battles of life. Our actions are merely a reflection of what is in our mind. We now understand we have the power over our greatest oppressor; fear.

Don't you feel good when you exercise the power of choice in your life?

Who chose the food you ate at the restaurant? Who chose the shoes you wore today? That's just it. Did you know, that fear is a choice? All our emotions are choices. Now you're asking, *"Timothy; are you telling me that I can change my mind about my fears"*? Yes!, yes!, yes! Absolutely yes. Choice is the gift of life and you have the power to use it and change things. Are you a robot? If the answer is no, then exercise the greatest gift of your life; making choices. You can triumph over your insecurities, by choosing courage and not fear.

Conclusion

"For I know the thoughts that I think toward you, saith the LORD, thoughts of peace, and not of evil, to give you an expected end". The Bible

The thoughts we should strive for are thoughts of peace. Insecurities, fears, anxiousness and stresses in our lives rob us of a peaceful state of mind. In these moments we ought to think of the thoughts God thinks towards us, thoughts of peace and a hope for the future.

"I learned that courage was not the absence of fear, but the triumph over it. The brave man is not he who feels afraid, but he who conquers that fear".

Nelson Mandela

Chapter Four: Self-Image

"Our self-image and our habits tend to go together. Change one and you will automatically change the other"
Dr. Maxwell Maltz

How do you see your-self?

The way we view ourselves will determine how we express our thoughts and body language to others. The way we see ourselves will also determine how much or how little insecurity we have. By now you can tell attitude is confidence, but the reason we struggle with our attitude is because of our insecurities. We also now begin to understand our insecurities are fueled by our negative self-image. In this chapter we will be dealing with the perspective we have about ourselves and how we project our perspective about ourselves on to others.

Our past experiences are like a mirror reflecting the good and bad things we've picked up along the way. A lot of what we believe about ourselves could be attributed to our childhood experiences and other major life experiences. When we adopt a negative self-image, we experience countless difficulties. If children are told they are ugly, they believe it and will be affected by it, unless they come to realize their true self-image. Likewise when a negative self-image is adopted and we are told negative things about our image by our friends, loved ones or even strangers, we are quick to adopt and run with it as truth. We can change all of this, by changing the negative images into positive images.

Self Confidence is all about perspective

Perspective is much like the lens on a camera. The photographer will adjust the lens until he has a better perspective. The truth is, the image the photographer wants to capture is perfect, but the photographer needs to zoom in or out, turn the camera sideways or adjust the lighting to get the perfect image the photographer wants. A photographer cannot use a lens made for nature or sport photography to capture a wedding portrait. This is exactly what we try to do. We don't realize that the picture is perfect already. All we need to do is adjust our perspective about ourselves in our own minds; instead we try to change the picture.

Why do you feel more confident when you lose weight, more daring with a set of new clothes, more approachable with a new hairdo? The answer is actually quite surprising. The way you see your-self has changed. When your self-image changes you see yourself differently. Why do we allow the external factors outside to influence your attitude rather than the real you; the internal person? Chances are that when we put the weight back on, all the insecurities will return and miserable feeling and low in confidence will become normality once more.

The main issues affecting us today when it comes to true confidence is not so much our weight or external features. In truth when we don't accept ourselves, we vent our frustrations on others as they only highlight what we already believe about ourselves. They say what we project, and that's not what we want to hear. We allow others to define who we are by giving people the power over us. We do this by paying attention to their negative comments and attitudes towards us. When you allow others to define you, you become a slave to the opinions of people.

As long as you see your-self through the eyes of others and not your own, you'll never be able to change the image in your mind. The life we live is a result of the way we look at ourselves. Your self-image is what you sell to the world. The true attitude of confidence can only become a reality when your internal conflict has been resolved. You can only be truly confident when you identify your low self-image triggers and change the way you see your-self. See yourself the way God sees you. Complete. Perfect.

We are not our behaviors. Whatever you've been doing till now, has been your choice. It should be a delight for you and I to know since all the negative behaviors were all our own choices, we can now change those choices into positive behaviors, but only if it is our own will to do so.

Self-Criticism

Did you know we all have a PhD in this subject? PhD - meaning *"Professional Hating Degree"*. Isn't it amazing how much energy we channel into criticizing ourselves? We've become professionals at hating ourselves. We hate our hair, our complexion, our figures, our height and weight. We take part in endless diets, buy equipment to work out in our homes and we never use it, take out gym memberships and only go to gym the first three weeks of the year. We relax our hair and put on extensions or get body tans because we are so dissatisfied with ourselves.

Consider for a moment if you were the only person in the world and there were no one to criticize or complement you, would you really care about making even the slightest change to your appearance? Probably not; I will tell you why, because the external influence wouldn't matter one bit.

How many critics do we have today?

Firstly; there's the inner critic. This is when you criticize yourself. You don't need any help. You do it all by yourself. This normally comes from your own insecurities planted by you in your life experience.

Secondly; there's the outer critic. This is when others criticize you. There's a saying that goes: "*In every criticism, there is a measure of truth*". I agree with the statement, however, it's not what people say, it's what you believe about what they are saying that counts.

Dr. Phillip C Mc Graw in his book *The Ten Life Laws* writes: *"No matter what the situation, you choose your reaction, assigning meaning and value to an event. ... You either teach people to treat you with dignity and respect, or you don't"*.

The only person who can allow others to criticize you is you. You give people power over you when you give too much attention to their criticism. A smart person will ignore them and take only the things you can build on from it.

Life Changing Questions:

- When will you decide *"I am better than this and that I deserve more than the scraps others define me by?"*
- When will you decide that you are the only one with the power to define you? The answer is a Loud and Resounding: NOW!

You are already perfect and there's is nothing wrong with presenting yourself even more beautifully than you already are, however, you should be the only one to decide. Remember, you teach people how to treat you. Love yourself and set an example to the world of how they should love you.

How should I see myself?

"The spirit of man is the candle of the LORD, searching the inner most being" The Bible

We are filled with light and with goodness and we should make every effort to reflect our light, rather than our darkness. We can only reflect what is within us. We carry the light of God in us. This light is the very life substance we have. It shines brighter than our self-doubt, but we must give it the chance to shine. How? See the light of God in You. We are the reflection of God. Perfect.

"*The darkness cannot overwhelm the light*". The Bible

Conclusion

"*There are two ways of spreading light. To be the candle or the mirror that reflects it*". Edith Wharton.

Switch off the voices of the critics in and around you, by elevating the right voice. Our entire Identity is based upon God's Image within us, and that is what makes us resilient. Focus on the right image and see yourself as God sees you. Perfect. (*Bishop Dr. SJ Lloyd*)

Chapter Five: Run Your Own Race

*"Therefore then, since we are surrounded by so great
a cloud of witnesses [who have borne testimony to the
Truth], let us strip off and throw aside every
encumbrance (unnecessary weight) and that sin which
so readily (deftly and cleverly) clings to and entangles
us, and let us run with patient
endurance and steady and active persistence the
appointed course of the race that is set before us". The
bible*

One of the most difficult things to do in this life is to learn the discipline of the race. The key to success is not running the race as such, but running your own race. Ussein Bolt the fastest man on the planet has taken part in the 2008 and 2012 Olympic Games, won all his races and set new world records as a result of one thing; running his own race. When he gets on to the track he forgets about everybody else and focuses on what he came to do. He forgets about the press conferences, all the "he said she said" nonsense and completely blocks out the world when the time comes to run. When he's on the track, he has one goal in mind, and the goal is to run his race the way he knows how. Setting records and winning medals is a bonus, but the ultimate prize is to be successful at running his race.

I will never forget something the great Australian cricketer Ricky Ponting said. The Australian team was making their way towards the changing rooms and the media asked some questions about the readiness of the team. Ricky got off the bus and said "*we have come to win the world cup*". I was amazed at his direct approach and frankly what he said, but I realized later he made a very powerful statement. He made a self-fulfilling prophecy. All the other captains and coaches from the other countries rambled nonsense like "*well, we are going to play our best and hope for the best*" or "*We have prepared well and there's a good spirit in the team*" or "*were hoping to get a good result*", but Ponting and his men had a single purpose their minds and they were not afraid to pronounce their mission to the world. Of course this was also a mental tactic to intimidate the competition and cripple their faith in themselves. It's no surprise to me they won that world cup that year. They did something profound, they went to the West Indies and played their game, they ran their race.

Repent From Otherness

E Bernard Jordan in his book *The Laws of Thinking* writes on the subject of otherness. He says anything that's not God is Otherness. In other words anything that's not for your Good is otherness. When I run someone else's race or meddle in their lane, I am living in otherness. Anthony Williams once asked me "*Tim, what do you think is repentance?*" I replied, "*well repenting is (re) going back to (pent) - highest point you were in your God Consciousness*. He liked my description and uttered these words. "*Repentance is a Change of Mind*". Before you and I can really begin to run our race, we must make a 360 degree decision. This decision is a complete change in our mindset. We should refrain from running and meddling in the races of other people. Run your own race and learn how to navigate your own path. God himself will cause unimaginable blessings and wisdom to come into our lives when we run our own race. We will run longer, harder, faster and further if we can stay in our own lane.

My Story

I was less than a year married and doing okay in my Job as a Financial Planner. After a few months we started having some challenges with the car we had and I felt I had enough of struggling with a car breaking down every so often. In our social circles my friends were doing quite well for themselves and buying new cars was on everyone's to do list. Guess what I decided to do; I decided that it was time to buy a new car as well. I was on a commission earning job, with no secure monthly income. Although I made good money at the time, it was an uncertain time in the economy. Despite all these factors I thought of the glory and satisfaction buying a new car would bring. After some deliberation I convinced Lizelle that we should do it and we went for it.

For the first few months everything went well, I was on top of the world and making money. In the months to come things became difficult. The insurance market dried up and things became even more testing financially. It was so bad at one point that I had to borrow money from my sales manager just to see a few clients and try to make sales. At one point we couldn't even afford to pay the electricity bill eventually plunging us in dark for three months. We were living on less than $22 a week and struggled. Eventually we had to get rid of the car. I realized later that I was not my friends and I was not ready to buy a new expensive car, not by a long shot. I tried to run everybody else race leaving my own and got myself into the situation.

Be Honest with Your-Self

The best thing you and I can do for ourselves is to be honest with ourselves. Isn't it amazing how we manipulate ourselves to satisfy temporary desires? We do this many times to our own detriment without really considering what the cost is. When life gets hard we are tempted to make hasty decisions that ruin us in the long-term. We can overcome these situations, but only if we take ownership and examine ourselves at these cross roads.

While sitting with my wife in a hair salon, I read an interesting sign on the wall. The sign read; "*what is this situation teaching me now?*" I was so taken up with this, I asked the owner why she put it there and she obliged saying "*when life gets tough I am reminded that I am a student of life.*" We cry, we complain, we say "*Lord why me?*" and yet the answers to the most difficult questions lie within ourselves, sometimes right on our doorstep.

When it gets tough to breath and it feels like the world is closing in on me, I ask myself "*God; what are you teaching me through this situation*". Not an easy question, but a question that always brings light and understanding to me. Once we discover what the situation is teaching us, we can take the lesson and apply it. There's a saying that goes "*when life gives you lemons, make lemonade*". Lemonade is a combination of three ingredients. They are lemon, sugar and water.

- First: Lemons - the **difficulties** in life.
- Second: Sugar - the **joys** in life.
- Third: Water - the **life** itself.

Life gives us the opportunity to blend these three life elements together and create something positive out of it. Pastor Virginia Botha always says: "*it's not what you go through, it's how you handle it*". Handle it with care, handle it with integrity and see the sugar not just the lemons.

Our way out is in being honest with ourselves about where we are, how we got there, and taking full responsibility. When we do this we unveil the learning in the situation. Ask yourself "*God; what is the lesson in this*?" No matter what you are working through, the message in the experience is more valuable than the mess. You will be liberated when you get the message.

"*Smart People also Make Bad Choices when their priorities are out of sync*".

Dr. Phillip Mc Graw

Why do intelligent people make bad choices? The answer is a simple yet complex one. Smart people make bad choices because we focus on the wrong priorities. We have the facts in front of us and we know what's in our best interest over the long-term, and yet we go ahead and make bad choices anyway. We focus on instant gratification as children do. "I want what I want, and I want it when I want." We are all tempted with 'now' glory in a situation and sometimes end up making bad choices, because we missed the mark. The mark is to understand what the real priority is.

We should constantly ask of ourselves, "What is my priority?" In other words what should get the most attention and why? What is the most valuable thing to consider in this situation? The question I should have asked is, whether my priority was to see clients or to drive a new car. Sounds simple, but the right answer could've saved me a lot of financial challenges. The priority was to build my business to the point where the business would have enough clients and collect enough passive income to pay for the new car. My priority should have been to see more people, not on how I arrive at a meeting. Today I make a lot of money without even leaving my office. My priority is to do the right business activities, not how I get around to appointments.

I remember having a conversation with Preneshen sometime ago and he said something profound. He said "I can get in a taxi and see clients and I will still close the million deal, because the client hardly ever sees my car." I agree with him, our success does not depend on the things we have, i.e. a nice car; it depends on how we present what we present when it matters. Since I started selling for a living, only a hand full of clients ever walked me out to my car. By now we gather we are able to make the best choices when our priorities are right. So go ahead and ask yourself; what is my priority? The best thing that we can do for ourselves is, run our race keeping in mind our own priorities.

The Way to the Top

When my previous CEO Nick True visited the country, I spent the day with him. Together we attended a number of meetings giving me the opportunity to observe his people skills. I had an interesting conversation with him, a conversation I will never forget. I mentioned to him South Africa being a popular destination for investors and entrepreneurs all over the world. My concern was South Africans would never realize their own potential and would always suffer from mental colonialism. I continued to say we would always be slaves and never live in true liberty and economic freedom for as long as we are asleep to our own potential.

Being a pearl of wisdom in his own right, Nick asked me if I wanted to know what the best advice was he ever received. I thought, this must be the advice that helped him build a global marketing agency. I replied, "*Please share, I would love to know*". Nick then replied by saying: "*the best advice I ever received was from my mentor and role model, my father. Do you know what my father said to me*?" He asked and I said "*yes?*" He answered, "*My father said to me Son; there's Plenty of Room at The Top.*" This blew me away, because for a moment I imagined the mental maturity at the top. At the top there is no scraping the pot, at the top there's an understanding of abundance. At the top they think in overflow, there's more than enough to go around. I realized that day; there is a place for me at the top. I would like to say to you, there is a place for you at the top.

How do I run my own race...?

There's really only one way to run your own race, and it has to do with discovering your life's purpose. When we know what our life's purpose is, we tend to ignore all the superficial junk such as position and material wealth and we start putting our Passion and Compassion into work. When we do this, position and material wealth becomes an automatic bonus.

Oprah Winfrey once said these words: "*Find out how you can get paid doing what you love*". She also said "*when you do what you love, you will never work a day in your life*". This is what our life's purpose is all about. We need to discover what we love, prepare and just do it. Life is too short to wait around. Every action in thought or deed will contribute towards fulfilling our unique purpose. We all have to come to a place in our lives where we stop running around being foolish and constantly looking for a quick fix or a quick bug. Let us run the Race with Patience, as God ordained it before the foundations of the world...

Answer the following questions as honestly as possible and see the clarity you receive.

Am I currently running my race where my Health, Money, Relationships, Passion and Compassion are concerned?

- Who's race am I running and why (who am I comparing myself to and why)

  _____

- When will I understand that I am different and unique?
  (Right now is a good time to start)

  _____

- When will I take my life back and value my own unique life experience?
  (Right now is a good time to start)

  _____

How do I discover my Life's Purpose?

By virtue of you being on this planet, you are a living breathing purpose. Life purpose has to do with filling the earth with the uniqness only you possess. It's about filling the earth with the life being, life doing and life having; giving that is authentically you. For me, that means cultivating within my being, doing and having; giving Love and Hope with all my thoughts, words and actions daily. My desire is be an influence in the shift towards a higher God Consciousness in the earth; to See as God, to Love as God, to Be as God and ultimately to Serve others as God. What is it for you? Only your inner most being knows.

What is pertinent is not just being already a living purpose, but having an impact as a living, breathing and doing purpose. Impact is the highest evidence of purpose. I have to inspire and create change. My purpose has its highest value when I contribute and participate in enriching the value of others.

We are for others, not just for ourselves. Some people are so rich, all they have is money or should I say some people are so poor all they have is money? There's so much more to life than doing for the purpose of having. Purpose is when you do for the purpose of being in complete oneness with God. Being in complete oneness with God is having the peace and fulfillment that can only come from serving others. Purpose is ultimately about serving away from your-self.

There are Four Pillars on which our life's purpose is built upon:

Pillar1. My life's Purpose is connected to Good

"For we are his workmanship created in Christ Jesus for good works, which God prepared beforehand, that we should walk in them". The Bible

Our life's purpose is connected to *good*. There is no *good* without God and so if your desire is to do good, you can rest assured that you are on track to doing a 'God thing'. To fulfill our life's purpose is a good thing. It's a God thing to live out your purpose and express the being that you are, the strength, hope and courage you are. What good thing do you love doing? Everybody has at least one good thing they love doing. This is the best place to start in discovering your life's purpose. If you have five good things you love doing you are on your way.

Some people love to make things with their hands; they find it therapeutic to work with their hands. Others are natural care givers, they love to work with children, or the elderly or as a nurse, doctor, physiotherapist, counselor and others in business or in other fields such as engineering etc. There are thousands of good things one can do, but what good thing do you love to do?

Think about five good things you like to do and note them down here:

1._____

2._____

3._____

4._____

5._____

Pillar2. I have a Special Ability

"*Your gift will make room for you*". The Bible

Acknowledge the gifts, talents or special abilities you have. I know many wonderfully talented people with different natural gifts to do or be something. One such person goes by the name of Preneshen. Of all the sales people in the world I know, he is one of the best. Preneshen has the ability to sell sand in the desert and he enjoys every second of it. Preneshen closed more than $2 000 000 of business in his last financial year alone, making him one of the best Marketing Directors in their niche sales promotion business.

"*A gift is as a precious stone in the eyes of him that hath it: wherever it turns, it prospers*". The Bible

Your talent or gift will take you far, but practicing discipline will keep you where the talent has brought you. We need to understand that success is 5% talent and 95% discipline

"*Genius is 1% inspiration and 99% perspiration*". *Thomas Edison*

The perspiration he spoke about is discipline. Discipline is a big part of one's character development. To develop character, we must apply force in the way we conduct ourselves and our affairs. For instance; if I know I am always late, I need to organize my thoughts and actions in a way that perpetuates punctuality. Your talent can take you to the stage of success, but discipline keeps you there and takes you to even higher platforms.

Pillar3. Your Talent is not your Purpose

"Talent will take you to the stage of success, but discipline will keep you there and open even greater doors" (NMC)

Your talent or gift is not your purpose, but it is a tool to help you fulfill your greater purpose. Let's use Preneshen as an example: Preneshen's purpose is not selling, but selling will help him achieve his greater purpose in life, which might be to become a global business leader helping to develop entrepreneurship in Africa, which in turn creates much-needed small businesses and business skills such as selling. This would help people become independent from the government and create a sustainable income for themselves.

His purpose as a family man might also be to create opportunities for his children and help his wife fulfill her own goals. Our Talents and Gifts are tools we possess to serve us. What we need to do is to acknowledge our natural abilities and evaluate where, when and how they could assist us for our greater good.

Pillar4. The Four Arrows of Purpose

We need to understand that our Purpose is a process of discovery based on four arrows. There is no waste in life only mistakes and experiences that have made us rich with wisdom. The four arrows will help point you in the right direction.

Passion ➡ Compassion ➡ Wisdom ➡ Timing

The First Arrow 1: Passion

Your passion is the one thing you really love doing. No matter where you are, you're always drawn to it. If you're not doing it, you are only half alive, but when you're living out your passion you experience joy and fulfillment. My passion is speaking. I discovered this 10 years ago while teaching life skills at a high school. Someone once asked me "*when were you most fulfilled in your life*"? I thought about the question and I recalled the moments I was working with high school children as a volunteer, teaching life skills. It was a while before I figured out that speaking was something I was naturally born to do. In all my previous banking, insurance and marketing jobs people were always drawn to me. I would always be the coach, the counselor and the one to speak to. People would always come to me if they needed advice or a pep talk. They always believed that I could rid anyone of their negativity and help them see the bigger picture. Colleagues always told me that I was in the wrong line of work. I finally decided to follow my passion and equip myself with the skills to be the best coach I could be and today you are reading my passion.

Your passion is the light inside you giving you the greatest joy. In the days I felt depressed or frustrated; my day would light up the minute an opportunity came for me to speak to someone. The moment I open my mouth and live out my passion, a fire starts burning inside of me and I suddenly come to life. Your passion is able to pick you up, when nothing or no one else can.

Passion is not delusion. I once asked a corporate executive what his passion was and the reply I got was "*my passion is making money*". I then I asked him if you had all the money in the world, what would you do for free? The answer, "*I will just spend that money*". This is not a passion, this is delusion. Delusion will cause you to think of your dream life without effort and meaningful labour towards an effective end. Passion is not a selfish activity, but something that brings joy to you and to others and it is work and fulfilling at that. What will people miss most about you?

People who really know you will miss your passion. Someone who has passion for soccer does not necessarily have a passion for round ball, but for what soccer can do. For instance: the sport can get kids off the streets and into a positive environment or create an environment where friends and family can fellowship. In both instances, it's the positive impact soccer has on a person that stands out. What is your passion?

Life changing question

Think of a day you were most fulfilled and note here:

_____

The Second Arrow 2: Compassion

Compassion: what do you really care about or what hurts you? Where can you show mercy and kindness? My compassion is people. I love people and I love helping people to overcome themselves. I am compassionate about this, because I too did overcome, and have constantly overcome myself. We are and will always be the biggest obstacle in our lives and my mission is to show people how to change their thinking and live; not just survive.

Ultimately I believe everyone's compassion should be around serving in some way or another. Some people serve the people while others serve in conserving animals or the environment. When there's nothing else left in the world, the only important thing will be the preservation of life. When we care about others, we show God's heart to them and a door opens in them setting them free from their own darkness. You and I, are the only 'God' people can see in this realm. The question to you and I is, "Are you able to show mercy to others and reflect God?"

What can you offer people in order to make their world better? Might just be a hug, a conversation, an ear to listen, this alone can touch a heart or make someone feel important. Most people never understand that we are here for one another, placed here by God to be kind. The most successful people in the world understand compassion to be the door to a life without limits and joy. So open your heart and ask your-self what and who do I care about.

Life changing question

What and whom do your really care about? Note here:

_____

The Third Arrow 3: Wisdom

"Wisdom is the principal thing; therefore get wisdom and in all thy getting get understanding". The bible

In other words gather what is most import in life; Wisdom. Wisdom is the principle thing meaning wisdom is the most important thing. Wisdom is knowledge, understanding and experience. For the Wright Brothers to be successful in building their plane, they needed Knowledge (what they wanted to do), they needed Understanding (what they could and couldn't do and why) and they needed Experience (knowing how to as they had learned from their failures' feedback). The key ingredient to wisdom is really experience.

Experience is the most expensive ingredient needed to propel you to your greatest successes. No university can teach you the practical part of business or medicine or even being a spiritual leader. The power experience offers unto us is the opportunity to learn from our successes and failures, and to use the insight we've learned to guide us to even greater success. Experiencing something is the best learning curve and these life situations become our best teachers in life. Value your experience and use it to your advantage when you have the opportunity to do so.

Reflection

What wisdom (knowledge, understanding and experience) have you gathered from the most difficult and most victorious moments in your life? Reflect for a moment the wisdom you have gathered in the following and note it accordingly.

Spiritually

Most	Difficult	Moments

_____

Most	Victorious	Moment

_____

Career

Most   Difficult   Moments:

_____

Most   Victorious   Moment

_____

Business

Most   Difficult   Moments:

_____

Most   Victorious   Moment

_____

Relationships

Most   Difficult   Moments:

_____

Most   Victorious   Moment

_____

Emotional wisdom

Most   Difficult   Moments:

_____

Most   Victorious   Moment

_____

Other

Most   Difficult   Moments:

_____

Most   Victorious   Moment

_____

The Fourth Arrow 4: Timing

"There's no such a thing as time management, you need to manage your-self around time" Joshua Mtanyelwa

Imagine what life would be like if the sun came up at 1pm every day and went down at 5pm. There'd be less than 5 hours a day to do things only possible during the day. In reality time is precious, limited and most expensive. We only have a short space of time to accomplish our goals. People who wait forever will allow their season for what they needed to do to pass and regret waiting around or on God for the right time. God is waiting on us. This is the excuse I hear from people all the time. Life is waiting on us to find ourselves, prepare ourselves and live our purpose. If time is so precious and we have so little, doesn't it make sense to live life to the full and follow your heart?

What's most important though; is to understand when the right time is for you to do. Can you imagine what would happen if a baby was born four months into the pregnancy? The baby would be still-born as the vital organs such as the lungs are not fully developed to cope with the outside world. Just because you're pregnant, does not mean it's time to go into labor.

In the same way, just because you are smart and full of potential does not mean you are ready. A great idea is never enough, nor is amazing talent. We need the experience element of wisdom to mature us for when the season to step out comes. We need to be mature before we are ready to take on the world. Are you responsible and faithful in small things? If you are you are maturing. If not, keep working on mastering your efficiency and faithfulness in small things.

"Maturity does not come by age, it comes by responsibility"
Author Unknown

How do you know it's your time? You will know it's your time when you've outgrown your space and your mentor believes you are ready. Mentor? "What do you mean mentor, I don't need people telling me what to do". It takes a father to call out the man in his son or a mother to call out the woman in her daughter. It simply means that they recognize your maturity and commission you to become responsible for yourself.

A mentor is a person who can help you get to where you want to go. Someone who will keep you accountable, coach you and help you make good choices to succeed. Your mentor should be a great deal further in life, than where you are and should have achieved more than you. Your colleague at work earning the same as you do and doing the same job you do is not your mentor, simply because they are where you are in life.

Mentors must have a proven track record, passion, compassion and the wisdom to inspire you. It is advisable to get a mentor in your life, I have several mentors. Some I connect with one on one, while I connect with others through their books, cd's, workshops and seminars. When you get a mentor you will see the value in having someone to support you with wisdom and passion and take you beyond where you've been before.

Learn to serve and become brilliant at your passion. Learn from your experiences and the experience of you mentors. When you learn from their wisdom, we leverage their expertise. This will help you avoid speed bumps and get to your life purpose destination faster.

Consider your timing carefully. When we're matured enough to accept a "*NO*" even when we want a "*YES*", we are on the right track.

Reflection Time

Have you ever done something prematurely? What have you learned?

_____

Have you ever procrastinated and missed an opportunity? What have you   learned?

_____

Next steps

If we want to run our own race, we need to connect with our Greater Life's Purpose. Our thinking should be around running our race with patience and growing our capacity to fulfill our innermost desires. Confidence is ultimately linked to what you are convinced about concerning your life's purpose. We all have a purpose and that thought alone should give us the courage to put on the attitude of confidence.

Passion + Compassion + Wisdom + Timing = Purpose.

All these arrows will help to point you to your destiny. Purpose will multiply your Confidence as you do what is true to you.

Conclusion

Running your own race accelerates your growth in confidence.

(Bishop Dr. SJ Lloyd)

Chapter Six: Emotional Intelligence

"Even though a high IQ is no guarantee of prosperity, prestige, or happiness in life, our schools and our culture fixate on academic abilities, ignoring the emotional intelligence that also matters immensely for our personal destiny."
Daniel Goleman

The concept of Emotional Intelligence has been around since at least the 1900's, but the term was first introduced by Wayne Payne in 1985. Emotional Intelligence was made popular by Daniel Goleman's Book called 'Emotional Intelligence' in 1995.

I believe if we strip the concept bare we will find a simple understanding. Emotional intelligence is our ability to master our emotional state and be aware of the emotional state of those around us and respond appropriately.

If we can't control our emotions we often create disaster around us. I like the example Paul Consalves made about anger. He spoke about the incredible Hulk. When he gets angry he loses control over his rational thought. He then grows with his anger and results in him becoming a green monster 10 times the size of a human being. Hulk goes on his path of destruction killing and destroying anything in his way. When it's all over he's comes back to his senses and realizes there's nothing he can do about all the destruction and pain he caused others. It's too late to rectify the situation.

In order for us to conquer ourselves, we need to understand ourselves better than ever before. We are the most advanced, most sophisticated and most dynamic generation ever experienced. We have to learn to master our emotions to live a balanced life.

What is an Emotion? (The Scientific Explanation)

An emotion is described as a physiological response to a situation too important to leave to intellect alone, such as danger, painful loss, persisting toward a goal despite frustrations, bonding with a mate, building a family. In effect, we have two minds, one that thinks and one that feels.

Let's take a deeper look at how the brain responds to emotions.

Source: Dick Culver

There are eight basic emotions:

- Anger
- Fear
- Happiness
- Sadness
- Love
- Surprise
- Disgust
- Shame

Paul Eckman, head of the Human Interaction Laboratory at the University of California, has found that there are characteristic facial expressions to describe the first four of these, which have been found to be consistent in all cultures, including primitive ones with no access to the outside world.

We cannot remain in a high emotional state for long. Eckman states that the full heat of emotion lasts for just seconds. At a less intense level, we may have moods that last for hours or days. At an even more fundamental level, we all have basic temperaments that shape our view of life and our role in it.

Some people are naturally cheerful or optimistic, while others are negative or pessimistic. These temperaments shape our beliefs about ourselves and the world around us. Goleman suggests that a student with a positive disposition would see an 'F' on a math test as evidence that he needs to work harder, while another may see it as evidence that he is stupid.

As a foundation we need to understand life is about learning. We cannot learn without our emotions, lest we become robots with no feeling. Our emotions are here to serve us and help us to develop. Have you ever seen a convicted murderer with no remorse? Chances are that as a child the person never learned how to deal with and understand his emotions. Perhaps when he was sad or cried was told that man don't cry and was forced to suppress his emotions. As the years go by and habit of crime evolved, very little if any remorse was shown and eventually this person develops into an emotionless self-centered being.

When the emotions have been suppressed for this length of time, it is possible for you consciously dissipate into a numb thought with no real value to serve you. I believe now more than ever it is crucial to introduce the subject of emotional intelligence into our school system and teach our kids about their emotions. We are all emotional beings and we feel. We are not animals, but spirit beings living in a mortal body with a soul. Our Soul refers to our Mind, Senses, and Emotions.

How does the Brain process emotions?

Researchers like Eckman have identified the physiological process for the emotional rush. When an external stimulus is received by one of our senses (eye, ear, taste, nose, touch) it goes first to the thalamus, where it is translated into the language of the brain.

Most of the message goes to the neocortex (the seat of rational thought), where it is analyzed and assessed for meaning and appropriate response. If that response is emotional, a signal goes to the amygdala, a small almond-shaped region in the brain, to activate the emotional centers. But a small portion of the original signal also goes straight from the thalamus to the amygdala, allowing a faster (but less precise) response.

Thus, the amygdala can trigger an emotional response before the cortical centers have fully understood what is happening. The amygdala houses memories and response repertoires that we enact without quite realizing why we do so. This fast response can be lifesaving in desperate situations, but can also result in inappropriate action.

The amygdala matures very quickly in an infant's brain. The interactions between the infant and caretakers during the first years lay down a set of emotional responses, a blueprint for emotional life. More slowly, the neocortex evolves based on cognitive training. It is because of this more gradual and extensive development of the neocortex that human beings are capable of the higher levels of rational reasoning unique to our species. The connection between the amygdala and the neocortex is critical to the functioning of the human mind.

A brilliant corporate lawyer developed a brain tumor. When the tumor was removed, the link between the cortex and the amygdala was destroyed. Although he appeared just as bright in analyzing complex data, he lost his job and marriage because he could not make a decision. Decision making is tied to the emotions since it is value based.

A Review of Emotional Intelligence by Daniel Goleman: Implications for Technical Education As quoted by Dick Culver

Emotional Intelligence: My Explanation

Emotional Intelligence is our ability to control our emotions and be an observer in any situation. As an observer you are enabled to calibrate your emotions and that of others using delayed rational thought and remedy the situation based on an outcome based response. Think about it clearly and remove yourself from the emotional stimulus in order to propagate the best balanced response. Emotional intelligence should really be about choosing your battles wisely. Remember people are not their emotional behavior. When you knew better, you would do better.

One important quality of an observer is the ability to understand there are a number of impetuses underlying behavior. One such is the role our hormones play at any given time. Mood swings are often a result of hormones being out of balance. This occurs in both the male and female body. The observer will take this important factor into account when discerning how to proceed in any situation.

"Observation gives us clarity beyond thoughts and feelings" NMC

How to apply this practically

Step 1: Be aware of your own emotions.

Be honest with yourself about your true feelings from moment to moment. *"I really don't like this"*

Step 2: Think clearly about what outcome is in your best interest.

The hardest thing to do is to think rationally when your body tells you to respond emotionally. You can however choose. You have that much power if not more.

Step 3: Choose the right rational response.

Consider how to handle yourself not others. You can calm yourself down and think of the big picture. Example: when you become angry, a good decision in your view would be to vent anger on someone. The best decision is to be reasonable and mature. You can choose for that, not to matter anymore.

Step 4: Let it go. It's not in your best interest.

Self-encouragement is a powerful tool at your disposal. Maturity is not determined by how old you are, but how you handle pressing situations. The disturbances in life are not the focus. Focus on your goals in your life plan. Ask the question "h*ow will this emotion serve me and get me to my goal*" don't fall for the trap of temporary satisfaction. It often comes with long-term disaster.

Step 5: Observe others

When you recognize the emotions in people and they feel that you have their best interests at heart, they are more likely to feel included and will be open to finding solutions with you.

Step 6: Respond to the need.

Underneath the emotional behavior are people with real challenges, seeking real solutions. Be sensitive and seek a win-win solution at all times.

Our Emotions are not going to disappear tomorrow. We can't wish away our emotions or that of others, because we now know our emotions serve us. What we need to learn is the basic need underlying our emotions. Remember your emotions are there to be of service to you, it keeps you alive.

People Have Two Needs

1. Significance

"Everybody likes a compliment". Abraham Lincoln

Dale Carnegie one of the most influential men in the industrial age shared something mind blowing in his 1936 book; *How To Win Friends & Influence People.* Carnegie who was considered as the chief communicator in his time demystified the concept of human relations and brought light to the power in communicating in the right way.

The passage below paraphrases Carnegie in his best seller: *How to Win Friends & Influence People*

Dr. John Dewey said that the deepest urge in human nature is "*the desire to be important*". What do you want? Not many things, but the few that you do wish, you crave with an insistence that will not be denied.

Some of the things most people want include:

1. Health and the preservation of life
2. Food
3. Sleep
4. Money and the things money will buy
5. Life in the hereafter
6. Sexual gratification
7. The well-being of our children
8. A feeling of importance (*Significance*)

Almost all these wants are usually gratified, all except one. There is one longing almost as deep, almost as imperious, as the desire for food or sleep which is seldom gratified. It is what Freud calls "the desire to be great." It is what Dewey calls the "desire to be important".

Lincoln once began a letter saying, "*Everybody likes a compliment.*" William James said, "The deepest principle in human nature is the craving to be appreciated." He didn't speak, mind you, of the "*wish*" or the "*desire*" or the "*longing*" to be appreciated. He said the "craving" to be appreciated.

Source: Dale Carnegie: *How To Win Friends & Influence People*

The above was written in 1936 and shows us that the need to be important is alive and well. As people we all share one basic need, this is why we stay in relationships, in certain jobs or a business.

- Is it possible that married men go to strip clubs and pay someone for special attention they crave and no longer get in their own relationships?

- In a recent survey conducted amongst women who've cheated on the spouses, the number one reason for the extra marital affairs was the lack of attention from their spouses. A staggering 91% said their spouses never made them beautiful and sexy anymore. Chilling isn't it?

- Could it be that people join gangs because they feel part of a family or they enjoy feeling important amongst the brotherhood?

- Why would a 45 year old man traffic drugs from Paris to Italy when he has everything? His answer "*I became addicted to the adrenalin. I felt that I was doing something important, my skill to do it was important, I felt important*".

- Could this be the same reason why young woman all over the world swallow up to 2 kilos of cocaine or braid 5 kilos of cocaine in their hair?

- Of course we can continue with examples, but we need to understand, that there is a need under the behavior.

How far have you gone in your life to feel important? In trying to deal with other people's emotions we need to keep in mind that people are important and their basic need is to feel important.

We need to change our approach and realize how we treat people. We should treat people as they are; important. When we master this, we have won half the battle.

2. Understanding

"Seek first to understand than to be understood" Author Unknown

People don't want us to get involved in their problems; neither do they have a desire for anyone to solve their problems. They want to be understood. According to Daniel Goleman, A big part of Emotional intelligence is being understood. Often all that's needed is understanding. The right approach is always: "*I understand. I might not agree, I might not see it your way, it might even offend or irritate me, but I always do my best to understand*".

Emotional intelligence is all about first understanding a situation by putting yourself in the shoes of the person and then mentally stepping outside of the situation; handling the challenge by considering all the issues.

You can't make changes from the outside; you can only make changes from within. In the heat of things it is easy to lose your cool and become emotionally involved. We all do it from time to time, but the golden key here is to understand the power and control you hold over yourself; a power to master your own emotions in the midst of chaos.

Understanding makes the world go around. Understanding ends wars and conflicts. Understanding brings clarity to students in a classroom. Understanding keeps marriages together. Understanding is a pearl of wisdom. When we learn to understand we become wise. Understand what? That underneath all the layers and issues are people with dreams, visions and good intentions, trapped in their emotional disturbances. The process is not smooth and you might not always know how to go about things, but you and I owe it to ourselves and others to listen and try to understand.

Understanding is the most important aspect in any relationship whether it is a marriage, employee-employer relationship, family, friends, acquaintances, customer-vendor relationships and all other interactions we encounter daily. When we seek to understand the other person, we can align our emotional state to be sincere. When we seek to understand the other person, we learn to give others a hearing and listen to what they have to say, instead of jumping the gun with assumptions and accusation. When we seek to understand others we ask questions and gather needs before we recommend solutions. We fail sometimes, because we think we know everything.

Emotional intelligence is about putting people before things, people before tasks, people before deadlines and finally people before our own selfish gain. It's about knowing what, when and how to say the right thing and allow people to leave our presence feeling that they are better off.

Only when we learn to listen, we are entitled to be heard. We cannot even begin to understand others if we are unwilling to give our undivided attention in listening to them. When people are given the opportunity to relieve themselves of the load they are carrying, they are open to us.

The Intelligent Choice

"The relationship is more important than the argument". (NMC)

We often get involved in difference of opinions and sometimes even arguments, but have we considered that it doesn't have to go this far? An easy solution to this is to seek out *The Intelligent Choice*. The intelligent choice is often found in thinking about how to de-escalate the situation and move forward positively.

The intelligent choice starts with an intelligent question: *"Do I want to get emotionally involved or rationally engaged"*?

The intelligent answer is to get *Rationally Engaged*. This is when we choose Thought before Emotion. Our ability to Rationalize allows us the opportunity to withdraw ourselves from a situation and put the relationship before the problem in relating to the person. The dispute, difference of opinion or argument should never take precedence over the relationship. I often say to my wife, "*baby you are more important to me than winning the argument.*" When she has an issue with someone I remind her and she sometimes reminds me, that the relationship is more important than winning the argument. To rationalize is to slow down, pause and think. It gives us the opportunity to re-think or think over, remain calm and make every effort to resolve the situation rather than prolong it.

How?

One way to employ rational engagement of thought is in using the old count to ten method. The psychologist of old recommended counting from 1 to 10 before you respond, and in so doing de-escalating the situation by allowing enough time to think and respond with a calm approach. The choice is clear. We can decide to think our way through it for 10 seconds or adopt prejudice (prejudge the other person without listening) and become emotionally charged.

Our thought life controls our emotional responses. Every reaction originates from a thought. Assumptions have a way of creating chaos in relating to others. Assumptions are based on prejudice. Have you ever spoken to someone who has prejudice is their mind? This is the kind of person who never listens, they only hear want they want to hear. You might say "*I am educated*" and before you could finish they would say "*so we are not educated*". You wanted to say "*I am educated when it comes to this situation, because we were given emotional intelligence training at work*", but you were pre-judged by the other person and they created a perception. Let me say this here: If you are not given the opportunity to speak and finish your thoughts, you are not responsible for the perception someone else creates in their mind. Period!

Perception is the responsibility of the one who has the perception. It's our obligation to clarify what we perceive by asking and checking with the person we are speaking to. This should be our second option. Our first option is to give people a hearing. We have to continually expand on our thought life capacity, so that we are immune to getting emotionally involved in a situation. Disputes in business, partnerships, relationships, families and organizations often get to a point of no return, because of emotional decision making. When we prioritize emotionally charged decisions over rational decisions we create disasters that could've been avoided. We need to put people before arguments.

We can get so involved with our prejudice (prejudging others and believing that they are judging you) and often don't realize that we create these walls wherein we destruct ourselves thinking we're protecting ourselves. We become defensive at every turn, never giving anyone the chance to say something and when they do, we jump to conclusions in our mind believing the whole world is against us. In reality we are against ourselves, living with regrets and dealing with the repercussion of our mistakes thinking we are being judged. The only person we are constantly fighting is ourselves. We will be dealing with more of this in chapter seven.

If people do judge us, it's because we judge ourselves so harshly that we teach them how to judge us by our actions. Again we don't realize, it's all in our mind. If this is you; aren't you tired of fighting so hard to defend something that only exists in your mind? I remember when I was so self-involved; it was draining me and all those around me, until I learned to make better emotional choices.

Our thought life will continue to rule our emotions if we choose how our thought life contributes. An empty thought life charges emotional reaction while an invested thought life responds with rational thinking. Our thought life is like a bank we deposit money into and withdraw from. When we deposit enough, we can withdraw from it and solve problems rationally in times of crises. If not enough was deposited, we can become emotional and bombard the person, rather than the problem.

People are not the problem; people's behavior is problematic and sometimes extreme. It is important not to fight with people, rather to understand you're dealing with a mindset. This mindset will produce a certain behavior. The good news as we said before is that behaviors can change, but it starts with the beliefs in the thought life that needs change. It starts with you and me making *The Intelligent Choice; Getting Rationally Engaged*.

Conclusion

It should be our quest to seek a compromise and be compassionate through understanding others, that we earn the respect to be understood. (*Bishop Dr. SJ Lloyd*)

Chapter Seven: Self-Leadership

*"Self-leadership is not about managing life's chaos,
but about developing character". (NMC)*

Self-leadership is the ultimate reflection of true confidence. It is the internal quality that holds the key to confidence. If you can lead yourself, confidence becomes a byproduct.

Leadership is described by one of the world's foremost experts on the subject Dr. John C Maxwell in one powerful word; 'Influence'. If leadership is influence, then whom do we need to influence when it comes to self-leadership? The answer is simple, but not always obvious. Self-leadership is my quest to lead my thoughts, guide my words and commit an action with the highest integrity to fulfill my life purpose.

"Real leaders are not respected because of their title; they are appreciated for their excellence and the results they produce". (NMC)

They say respect is earned, but what would you rather have; Respect or Appreciation. There is a difference between Management and Leadership. Managers demand respect, leaders on the other hand is bombarded with appreciation. Management is a systematic approach to handle chaos, while Leadership is a systematic approach for development. Self-leadership always seeks the best way to continue development.

The self-leader is one who delivers. The self-leader produces results, not stories or reasons why they could not. The self-leader does not focus on managing life's chaos; they focus on developing their character. Their self-leadership is so strong; others can see it and are drawn to it without any external coercion. Those drawn to the self-leader appreciate the excellence they see and follow the self-leader. The self-leader's thoughts, words and actions are in perfect harmony.

Think for a moment of someone whose words and action never contradict. Think of the 'Go To' person for everything. They always have people around them. They are natural thinkers always asking questions and finding solutions. They are honest and give 100%. They pour their heart and soul into whatever they do. That is a strong self-leader.

The Self-leader is someone who silences their inner and outer critic by delivering results. It's about following through with a diligent sequence of harmonized thoughts, words and actions until their vision has materialized. Self-Leadership is about you leading you to think, say and do what is necessary with the highest level of integrity to fulfill the purpose.

The Battle for Supremacy

There is a battle constantly raging within. It is the battle for supremacy. This battle is always between your Higher Self (your life purpose) and your Lower Self (your weak self). The higher self is always looking to find reasonable agreement within and keep you on the road of purpose. It is your reason for existence and living. It is the substance of God that keeps you alive. We are all packaged with it. It is the license we have to occupy this space, in this realm, on this planet, at this time.

The lower self on the other hand wants to distract you from the purpose you are. It does this by feeding three life distractions. These are also known as the three sins.

The Lust if the Eyes:

What the eye sees and desires. Cluttering the vision and focusing on material possession in the place of one's authentic passion being followed. When life purpose is sidelined for material gain.

The Lust of the Flesh:

What the body, the hormones and emotions desire. Cluttering the authentic compassion to feel for others and choosing instant and selfish gratification over the fulfillment of one's greater purpose.

The Pride of Life:

Self-absorption and selfish gain becomes priority. The desire to be served and to prove supremacy over others instead of recognizing that we are all servants of each other. Neglecting my authentic purpose to serve others. Being out of place.

Which one would you consider a characteristic of your higher self?

Discipline or Procrastination _____

The self-leadership battle determines whom we serve. This is what we are all confronted with daily. Either way, my choice to lead the Right Self (higher or lower) determines whether I serve my life's purpose or my life's distractions.

By now you have some guidelines on discovering the authentic purpose that you are. Purpose is not something you do, it is ultimately who you are. Every thought, every word and every action is a reflection of who you choose to be at any given moment. If you walk in the purpose that you are, you are leading. If you are entertaining your life's distractions you are merely managing your life's Chaos. It is not enough to manage your mind, it is far more important to lead your mind. Self-leadership is then the quest to continually live a repentant consciousness. In other words; I constantly need to adjust my frame of mind to correct my thoughts, word and action towards achieving my Life Purpose.

I love the example of Jesus Christ. It's clear that he built his legacy by contributing significantly in giving himself completely to his life purpose and by choosing awareness. The world knows his name today because he is The Way; he showed The Way to do it.

To win the battle of supremacy we need to operate to our highest advantage. Living not just on the level of cognitive and emotional intelligence, but on the level of our highest self; the level of awareness. This is when you see all sides of a coin, the head, the tail and rounding of the coin. This is when you consider all the factors. Someone once said that there are two sides to every story and then there's the truth.

How do I practice more awareness?

- Seek the truth in everything
- Take absolutely nothing for granted and at the same time appreciate all the details. A picture is made up of millions of pixels, not one or a few. The self-leader makes choices based on the outcome, not the process.
- Choose to be an observer and order your steps according to your highest intention. Stop managing your life's chaos by feeding your three distractions. Give your attention to the thoughts, words and actions that consolidate your purpose, the being or spirit that you are.
- Every day presents a new opportunity for us to lead ourselves to our higher purpose. Forgive yourself, forgive others and focus on today. The way I see it, there are no mistakes only life lessons

that enrich my life and strengthen my character. I am a student of life. Awareness affords me the opportunity lead myself to my higher purpose daily.

Qualities to practice when leading myself

Invest in your thought life

As discussed, it's very important to invest in your thought life by constantly feeding your mind with options. Read, discuss, ask, research and most of all observe.

Have a Clear Vision

Maintain a clear big picture of what the end result will be. Make it as detailed as possible describing when, where, what, who, why, and how you are going to achieve it.

Apply Diligence

Diligence is the ability to work at it no matter what, and keep on until the end. To be reliable, and deliver at any costs. Someone who follows through and keeps going when it gets tough.

Strive for Excellence

Excellence speaks for itself. It means that we need to be effective in our action. Whatever we do in this life will be reflected in the results. The universe does not reward thought or feelings, life rewards action. The more effective we are, the higher we climb.

Love Humility

What is life teaching me right now? That is humility, being teachable. Leading yourself is the greatest learning curve as you learn patience through the difficult times life presents. We can also learn from the great times, however we become relaxed. If we listen carefully to the cosmos speaking to us in times of plenty, we would hear the sound of caution saying "store up!"; beware as life is always filled with balance. For every fat year, there might be a year of adventure or a year of discovery and sometimes difficulty. The prince of Egypt most certainly lived on a level of awakened awareness. Humility is a monitoring and evaluation tool. It helps us to stay in check.

Focus on the Purpose

The most profound of all these qualities is purpose. Will Smith the entertainment billionaire says "*I do nothing without purpose*". Purpose is a measuring stick. Purpose always reminds me what I'm supposed to achieve and why. It's so easy to get caught up in the spur of the moment, to lose track and slacken or even change direction, but I always ask myself "*what is the purpose of what I'm doing?*" Asking this question always puts me in front of my mission.

Chapter Eight: The Keys To Lasting Confidence

"Experience tells you what to do; confidence allows you to do it".
Stan Smith

What is the difference between human beings and animals? There are plenty differences. For one, animals can't talk; they don't build houses, planes, skyscrapers or technology. They have no desire to visit the moon or to cook, they don't love and they lack vision for the future. The reason is simple, they are animals.

We have Potential

"The potential of the average person is like a huge ocean unsailed, a new continent unexplored, a world of possibilities waiting to be released and channeled toward some great good." Brian Tracy

What we possess as Spirits, living and a mortal body is unlimited potential. The word potential is described in the dictionary as: *An unrealized Ability to do something.* Martin Luther King, Nelson Mandela, Barack Obama, Ussein Bolt, Natalie De Toit, Oscar Pistorius, Albert Einstein, Dale Carnegie, Henry Ford had the potential to be great. All they needed was to find or create opportunities to meet their potential. Did they succeed? Of course, otherwise we wouldn't have known their names today. Just like all these people, you and I already have the ability to accomplish anything we invest within mind. We should realize we can do it and believe in our own abilities. Your potential is your treasure, your blueprint. No one knows what you are capable of except the Spirit living within you.

We are different

Potential is what separates us from animals. We dream, we envision and strive towards something. We live in faith and with hope conquering ourselves within and the obstacles life throws at us, because we have the potential to do it. Potential is the most powerful force for change.

When we begin to understand how to harness our potential, we are free to conquer the world. Confidence is based on a conviction. The most confident people in the world are convinced about an idea, and this idea is what gives them the power to persuade others, as they are persuaded about the Idea. For instance a woman selling a slimming product she used to lose 100 pounds successfully will be extremely confident about sharing this with others, because she is persuaded the product works. In the same way, when we are convinced about our potential, we have already won half the battle.

Conclusion

"*Stir up the gift of God which is within you*" The Bible

Think about the following scenario:

When buying real estate in desperate need of renovations and you pick it up below the market price, the best reason to consider investing in the real estate is the potential it has. You might not appreciate the immediate value, but it has the potential to grow into a substantial asset. So too; we have been packaged with so much potential to fulfill our destiny. (*Bishop Dr. SJ Lloyd*)

Live in the Realm of Possibility

We often allow thoughts of self-sabotage and fear to grip our hearts instead of taking courage and focusing on what's possible. Using the worst case scenario is the worst self-sabotage we can inflict on ourselves as we use thoughts, words, pictures and actions to create our own reality. We later wonder why we experience negative situations and never realize we created it. Consider the following; when you use the worst case scenario, you picture it and you're feeling about it ultimately create a negative energy which in turn produces the event.

Focus on the Possible

What we should be focused on, is the best possible scenario. In the same way, when we focus on what is possible, we stimulate positive energy creating positive experiences. Confidence is all about believing it's possible even if there's only a 1% chance. A wise person understands 1% is enough for a miracle. How many sperm cells are needed to breakthrough and fertilize an egg? Only one out of a few million cells can do it. How many women thought they would never get pregnant as they were on the pill or counting between ovulation or this and that and yet found life to be full of surprises? It is possible. Is it easy? Almost never, but it's possible. Remember the next time you are confronted with an impossible situation that anything is indeed possible. This is a lasting key to the attitude of confidence.

Thomas Edison the famous American inventor and businessman greatly influenced life around the world. He invented and improved many products including the practical electric light bulb. He was one of the first inventors to apply the principles of mass production and large-scale teamwork to the process of invention, he is credited with building the first industrial research laboratory.

Edison is the fourth most prolific inventor in history, holding 1,093 US patents in his name, as well as many patents in the United Kingdom, France, and Germany. What I like most about this powerful figure is his attitude towards what's possible. He was quoted saying: "*If I find 10,000 ways something won't work, I haven't failed. I am not discouraged, because every wrong attempt discarded is another step forward*".

We decide whether we experience failure or feedback. When we see our mistakes and failures as feedback, yet another door is open to possibility. Believe in the possibility even when it's tough.

Life is an Adventure

I don't like to use the word challenge in my vocabulary. I always hear people saying "*ooh I am dealing with so many challenges*". The word challenge is a self-fulfilling prophecy. Things become difficult because you give the universe the right to place obstacles in your way. I prefer to use the word adventure.

When do you feel at your best?

When do you feel at rest?

When do you feel excited to explore?

When you go on Holiday right!

This is one of those beautiful life moments. It happens occasionally but it's so profound when it does. Notice how you feel when you are going on the journey. You feel relaxed, at peace, grateful and excited. You don't have a care in the world because you are going on an adventure. You have no clue what the voyage will bring, but you feel blessed to get away from it all. Why? The approach makes all the difference.

One hundred cancer patients were notified about a new drug expected to have remarkable results within days. The hospital was to give this new drug in addition to the drugs the patient were already being treated with. Only a handful were excited to try this new drug, others remained pessimistic and cynical.

They were all given the new medication and within a few days cancer patients showed recovery as tumors decreased in size and some were up feeling better. After two weeks some were going home and others continued to recover during the same month, while other cancer patients given the same drugs got worse and some even died. What they did not know is that the medication they were given were placebos (a substance with no healing property) a blank capsule. What made the difference was the approach to the medication. Some saw the new drug as a new adventure, a new possibility, a new beginning. Others saw their pain and suffering.

"Your strength is determined by the size of your enemy" (NMC)

Life has a wonderful way of exposing your strength to you. Life will only give you obstacles you can overcome in great measure. The word adventure refers to a process of discovery. What discovery you may ask? The answer is quite profound: *Discovering your own strength.* Life is an adventure. We don't know what tomorrow holds anyway, you might as well keep your head up and look forward to the journey. Think of discovering not only the strength in you, but also the divinity in you. God in you... You are stronger than you will ever know.

Conclusion

"All things are possible to those who believe" and *"Nothing shall be impossible to you"* The Bible

Jesus showed us that absolutely nothing can stand in our way when we believe. Napolian Hill said; *"Whatever the mind can conceive and believe, it can achieve*". These powerful secrets emanate from the wisdom found in the scriptures. (*Bishop Dr. SJ Lloyd*)

Tip One: Confidence is an Art

The chairman of the previous company I worked for taught me an important skill in sales. It's called theater. I am certain he's taught all his staff all over the world this powerful concept and I believe many more marketers, sales and advertising minds can learn something here. He said to me *"Tim, when you master your theater, you will be far more successful"*. Nick believes that marketing and especially sales is about presenting the best possible performance to you audience. In this case the client.

When a performer goes on stage, they switch from being themselves to being the performer. Brilliant examples are Beyoncé Knowles, Lady Gaga or even the late Michael Jackson; capable of putting on their theater at any time. They become someone else. The best performers in the world can switch to their character and stay in that character for extended periods. This is what separates the pro's from amateurs. Theater is what they do. They prepare for their role as if it will be their last performance and they give their best on stage. They often if not always surprise and move the audience. Remember; people buy people and they buy you.

You and I are constantly on the stage of life. We are constantly selling ourselves to others and it's our job to move the audience. It's your mission to entertain and woo the crowd with motion, sound and emotion. You are constantly performing your master piece and nothing else is more important than staying in character. Nick taught us to be diligent in preparing before every meeting. Doesn't matter who you're meeting with, preparation is key. So the way to do it is to get you in the zone by staying in the car for a few minutes and relaxing yourself with deep breaths. Slow Deep breath in, Slow Deep breath out and doing this 3-4 times until you are relaxed. Then you need to focus on your persona. In other words who are you playing and what is the message you want to convey?

I'm sure you've seen the skills these professionals exhibit. How many times have you seen a theater piece or a movie and completely believed it was real, even when you know trucks don't really transform into super robots, but still the actors are so good at believing what they act, you and I believe it. If you are genuine and honest people will buy from you, but you have to put it on, just like we put on sunscreen on a hot sunny day. Why do performers like Will Smith, Denzil Washington, Julia Roberts and Jamie Foxx get paid well over 20 million dollars a movie? Because the directors and creators of the film know they can bring the script to life; and they do.

In 80% of all football matches played around the world the person who scores one goal will go on to score another goal during the match. The player is filled with the attitude of confidence after the first goal so much so that he believes he can score again and does so most of the time. He holds his composure, stays calm under pressure and follows through when he has the chance.

In the same way you and I have to put on the character of our most powerful self. The more you practice this, the more it becomes natural. Note: I am saying your best self, not anyone else, but you at your best moment. Think of a moment when you felt powerful, a moment you were without fear. Do you remember a moment you were unstoppable and full of life? Think of that moment the next time you need to go into character.

Tip Two: The 20 Second Rule

Preface

This book is not a dedication or praise in any way or form to Oscar Pistorius. Nor do I condone the taking of a human life by another. It saddens me that someone with an important life purpose has been cut off in the prime of life.

This book was originally written in 2012 before Oscar Pistorius was indicted for murder. At the time Oscar was a hero and an inspiration to billions of people all around the globe, hence I have decided to keep the original content in this chapter based on the spirit it was written in. We never know how people will turn out and what challenges they may face in their lifetime. We can choose to judge people on their best moments or at their worst moments, but is it for us to judge? Just because our dirt is not aired in public and splashed all over doesn't mean we are better than anyone anyway.

Marian Jones, Mike Tyson, Lance Armstrong, Tiger Woods and many others whose dirt has not yet been exposed have made one thing clear. Brilliance is not without vices. They chose to submit their will to their lower self as discussed in chapter seven. If anything these are the heroes whose lives speak of how not to give into our three distractions. I choose to let their best and worst moments teach me.

Is it better to judge or to learn from them? I would like to think that learning has highest value.

He is called the fastest man with no legs. He has fought many battles and come out on top every time. He is known to the world as the poster boy of Paralympic athletes. He is the world's fastest paralympic, a record holder and the champion of the 2012 Paralympics. His name is Oscar Pistorius.

What comes to your mind when you think of the blade runner Oscar Pistorius? One word comes to mind for me is; Brave.

Over the last 8 years he became known for his zest for life, his daring nature and his desire to be more than the world ever thought he could be. This athlete with no legs, who runs on blades, wanted more. He wasn't satisfied with only running against paralympic athletes; he wanted to run with able-bodied athletes. He fought and fought and fought yet again until the International Association of Athletics Federation gave in and allowed him to compete with able-bodied athletes. Oscar made history at the 2012 London Olympics by being the first blade runner to compete with able-bodied athletes at the Olympic Games.

When I look at his athletic career, something powerful springs to mind. It's called the 20 second Rule. It took Oscar many 20 seconds of bravery to accomplish what he has. 20 seconds on the track 20 seconds in the board rooms, 20 seconds in his training, 20 seconds in front of the IAAF and many other 20 second rule moments. I believe he needed to be brave for only 20 seconds at a time to achieve the miracles in his life.

20 seconds can change your life forever. I believe 20 seconds is the difference in sport games, business meetings, presentations, relationships, job interviews and so many other spheres of life. 20 seconds is a short time, but can have a profound impact on one's life. I never knew I was a believer in the 20 second rule, until I saw it in a movie and I instantly connected with the 20 second rule.

Serena Williams at the Wimbledon 2012 final applied the 20 seconds of bravery to fight her way back from number 175 in the world to become the 2012 Wimbledon Champion. The moment she said to herself "*I can do this*" a window of hope opened and she pushed her best self forward building her bravery second by second until she had the courage to fight back and win her 14th title.

The 20 second rule simply means to put on your best self for only 20 seconds at a time. When you're brave for 20 seconds at a time, you open a door inside you with no doubt, no fear and no uncertainty. Being brave for 20 seconds allows you to do the very thing that terrifies you as you transition from an un-resourceful state to a resourceful state. I must tell you the results I've experienced in my life are astounding. I remember using it when I met my wife and when I proposed to her. I remember using it in the biggest business presentation as an entrepreneur. I even remember using the 20 second rule to introduce myself to billionaire Patrice Motsepe in an impossible environment.

I have used the 20 second rule in the powerful Braintools Seminars helping people crippled by their fear of heights to get over the phobia. One lady leaped from the table to a chair, sliding to the floor and flipping the chair over without falling, and she was mortified at the thought of just getting on a table in the first place. I asked her afterwards to describe to the class how she did it, and she replied, "*I can do anything in my 20 seconds of bravery*".

I bet if you think about it, you can come up with many 20 seconds of bravery that brought you amazing results. Perhaps you swam with a shark, or jumped out of a plane, maybe you saved your life or someone else's life and recall you don't know what came over you. Perchance you told someone you love them and it developed in to a relationship, you might still be together today. Think of the 20 seconds that changed your life, I can almost guarantee you have one. How many miracles have you experienced when you were brave for 20 seconds?

The idea is not to be foolish and do something crazy. The idea is to understand you will be giving your mind a 20 second timeframe to dare and believe you can. Suddenly the divinity in you comes alive and the adrenalin rushes through your veins. When this happens you are ready to take on your giant. Don't you think David used the 20 seconds of bravery rule when he faced Goliath? I think he did.

The key is to put on your bravery as a shield and just do it. The word brave means: To show courage; to be fearless; to confront boldly; to defy. The only real fear you have, is the fear that you can do it and that you might actually surprise yourself. We don't like to be proved wrong. We would rather be right about rubbish like believing it can't be done, than risking and believing in the smallest possibility.

Some people are so stuck in their negative expectation of themselves that they feel safer staying in a cocoon. They prefer to live a predictable existence when life itself is so unpredictable. If you are one of those people who would rather play it safe, then I want to encourage you to take one small step of faith, especially when you feel like you can't. Life will surprise the hell out of you and bring you unexpected blessings. Start by challenging yourself and expect more from you.

The 20 second rule is like a secret weapon only to be used when you need to move higher in your expectation of yourself. It's the attitude of complete faith in you. People buy this, because guess what it is your true self. When you decide to use the 20 seconds of bravery to defy your situation, you bring out your innermost confident self. The 20 second rule allows you a platform, a reason to release the beast inside you.

How to use it?

Firstly and most importantly, you must understand you are brave already. Take a deep breath and see how you do what you are afraid of, in your mind. Then for 20 second just lose your mind and do it. Don't think, don't hope, and don't pray just take action. Do it again and again until you achieve.

Tip: Three: The Do's and Don'ts

How to handle yourself around others

- Looking people dead in the eyes is a sign of intimidation. No one likes this. Moderate eye contact is good enough and makes people comfortable.

  Guys; A woman knows when you are focused on her breast. Most women don't appreciate it, although there are those who crave attention and will put themselves out there in this way. Ladies when you do this you are unmasking your insecurities. You are more than that, you are better than that.

- A firm hard hand shake is seen by people as intimidating. Give a good handshake with a light grip. Be yourself and give a polite smile.

- Smiling too much and putting on false excitement is easy to spot. It's open like a book and people can see it. Rolling your eyes when someone else is talking is disrespectful and unfriendly.

- If you disagree, write down their comment and how you can address their concern. When the person you are talking to sees you are writing, they feel important. That is the goal. I don't care who you are or who your customers are, if you make them feel important they will feel that they owe you. At some point the client will recommend you. You show them that you recognize their presence and voice when you write what they say.

- When you are in a meeting, never sit if you have not been seated. This is their office, their space and they don't need you to invade it. Invasion is seen as arrogance and rudeness and people don't take kindly to it.

- Never see yourself to someone's office unless you were instructed to do so by them or their PA. Know your place, you are a visitor. Many people lose job opportunities, because they play buddy buddy with the interviewer or potential partner. Just because the person on the other end is nice or friendly doesn't mean they think of you as their best mate. They are not going to invite you to their house over the weekend or a manicure on Saturday, so keep it professional. Remember, professionals like professionals and professionals like to work with their own kind. You must establish early on what kind of person you are dealing with.

- **Important**: the only time you are allowed to say something is when you're asked or given the platform. Be direct, helpful, informative and genuine. People buy people.

- When you're standing, stand straight up and turn your body to the person you're addressing. This makes them feel that they have received information from someone who gave their question or comment consideration.

- Never interrupt the person speaking, keep your mouth shut and wait for them to finish. I have interrupted clients and lost sales, because I talked myself out of the business. Only speak when it's absolutely necessary and answer in detail so that they feel you know what you are doing.

- If you are a smoker, always you're your hands. Most non-smokers can smell smokers a mile away, because it is a foreign smell to them, unlike you the smoker who can't smell your smoking residue anymore. The last thing you want to do is make people uncomfortable around you.

- Power colors are Black, Navy or Dark Blue, Dark Gray, Gray and Brown. These colors vibrate competence.

- Ladies PLEASE..... Don't overdo the make-up. What you don't know is that everyone can see the white line separating your neck from your face. Avoid looking like a fake or a fool at all cost, be as natural as possible.

Conclusion

"All personal breakthroughs begin with a change in beliefs".

Anthony Robbins.

This is fundamental as our beliefs system is all build upon our value system. This program is intended to assist you into making this paradigm shift in reviewing and changing your beliefs.

Frank Zappa said "*A mind is like a parachute. It doesn't work if it is not open*".

As we think we are and constantly become. We are packaged with an extraordinary image. An image to create any outcome we determine within. Our thinking determines our final destination in every sphere of life. A positive attitude will enhance the passion and enthusiasm within us, which will in turn electrify those around us.

"*When you choose the behavior, you choose the consequences*". Dr. Phil

As you follow through with Confidence, Bravery and the Do's and Don'ts, great result will follow. (*Bishop Dr. SJ Lloyd*)

Terms of Use

This information is provided through various sources as information only and may not be construed as Medical or Psychological advice or instruction. Readers should consult appropriate professionals on any matter relating to their health and well-being. The information and opinions provided herein are believed to be accurate and sound, based on the best judgment available to the authors, researchers and contributors, but readers who fail to consult appropriate authorities assume the risk of any injuries or loss. The author, researchers, contributors, editors and publisher are not responsible for errors or omissions or injuries resulting directly or indirectly from the use of this information.

The Author

Timothy Lloyd also known as the *New Mind Coach* is a Motivator, Life Coach, Consultant and Author using the power of Neuro Linguistic Programming to inspire people from all walks of life. His thought provoking self-awareness approach makes deep personal breakthroughs possible. Timothy has a burning desire to see people's lives changed by the power that lies in renewing the Thought Life.

He presents powerful seminars and workshops that drive real change empowering people for new thinking, creative thinking and problem solving, learning, memory and emotional mastery. The information presented is enlightening and stretching, giving people the power to do more than they ever thought possible.

Bookings

timothyl@live.co.za

www.ingramcontent.com/pod-product-compliance
Lightning Source LLC
Chambersburg PA
CBHW081213020426

42331CB00012B/3016